PRAISE FOR

like. love. follow.

Courtney and Stephanie take a smart, savvy approach to social media marketing that yields terrific results for their clients. Readers will find practical, how-to advice that is refreshing, honest, and most importantly, WORKS!

—**Carrie Kerpen,** *CEO of Likeable Media and coauthor of Likeable Social Media Revised And Expanded*

Stephanie and Courtney completely understood that, as an entrepreneur, I needed to wear many hats, including running my company's social media platforms. They taught me how to strategically use social media to grow my business, and I have no doubt that readers will see real results from their instruction.

—**Joanne Barken,** *CEO of TheBach.com*

Working with Courtney and Stephanie of Socialfly, we were able to bring our social media platforms to the next level. By using their tactics, we increased engagement and tripled our Facebook following in less than a year. They helped us develop innovative strategies for growing our overall engagement and brand recognition across all of the major social media platforms.

—**Sarah Kugelman,** *CEO of Skyn Iceland*

like.

love.

follow.

like love follow

THE
ENTREPRENISTA'S
GUIDE TO USING

SOCIAL MEDIA

TO GROW YOUR
BUSINESS

COURTNEY SPRITZER & STEPHANIE ABRAMS CARTIN

FOUNDERS OF **SOCIALFLY**™

Published by Advantage, Charleston, South Carolina.
Member of Advantage Media Group.

ADVANTAGE is a registered trademark and the Advantage colophon is a trademark of Advantage Media Group, Inc.

Printed in the United States of America.

ISBN: 978-1-59932-635-1
LCCN: 2015950060

Book design by George Stevens.

This publication is designed to provide accurate and authoritative information in regard to the subject matter covered. It is sold with the understanding that the publisher is not engaged in rendering legal, accounting, or other professional services. If legal advice or other expert assistance is required, the services of a competent professional person should be sought.

Advantage Media Group is proud to be a part of the Tree Neutral® program. Tree Neutral offsets the number of trees consumed in the production and printing of this book by taking proactive steps such as planting trees in direct proportion to the number of trees used to print books. To learn more about Tree Neutral, please visit **www.treeneutral.com**. To learn more about Advantage's commitment to being a responsible steward of the environment, please visit **www.advantagefamily.com/green**

Advantage Media Group is a publisher of business, self-improvement, and professional development books and online learning. We help entrepreneurs, business leaders, and professionals share their Stories, Passion, and Knowledge to help others Learn & Grow. Do you have a manuscript or book idea that you would like us to consider for publishing? Please visit **advantagefamily.com** or call **1.866.775.1696**.

Dedication

*To all of our mentors, family, clients, and
incredible Socialfly team for all of your support and
encouragement on our entreprenista journey.*

To our mentor, business attorney, and friend, David Feldman.

To our copy editors, Greg Cartin and Mary Kate Hoban.

Table of Contents

About the Entreprenistas

COURTNEY SPRITZER

I grew up in a family of entrepreneurs. I've been surrounded by strong female figures my entire life—women who started their own businesses at a very young age without ever working in corporate America. Without a doubt, that shaped my way of thinking, but I still needed to forge my own path before I would join my family of business owners.

I studied business and economics at New York University (NYU). After graduating in 2009, I joined a management training program at a leading regional insurance company in Massachusetts and joined the bond underwriting team. My primary responsibility involved analyzing the risks associated with businesses in construction, telecom, banking, and other industries. In 2011, I moved back to New York City, where I went to work for American Express as a financial analyst supporting a marketing division. Both of these experiences have made me a stronger entrepreneur, as they gave me the insight I needed into how companies operate smoothly, given all the moving parts. Knowing how to manage money and having an understanding of corporate structure gave me the confidence I needed to enter the world of entrepreneurship.

Now let's back up a bit. When I began my college career at NYU in 2005, Facebook was only available to college students, and

I couldn't wait to sign up. For four years, I spent countless hours on the social network, as did most of my college peers. It was how I connected with new friends, stayed in touch with old ones, documented my college experience, and kept tabs on my college crushes. Little did I know this would lead to a career down the line.

If you were to know Stephanie and me, as partners, you'd think we were longtime friends. In reality, we met for the first time in 2010, when my best friend, Susie, introduced us. Susie had started her own company in college, and Stephanie had already started a social media agency. I thought it was an incredible concept. I knew that social media wasn't a fad. Even after college, it had remained a huge part of my life, and the landscape had evolved even more, with platforms such as Twitter and Instagram becoming important players in the industry.

At that time, I worked for Amex, which was becoming the social credit card. Amex formed partnerships with Facebook, Twitter, and Foursquare. I had a front-row view of a major company utilizing social media to provide a better experience for its card members. In 2011, Stephanie was searching for a business partner and I joined her to capitalize on what I now knew as fact: social media would be a powerful marketing tool for all businesses, both large and small.

Our company began as a side project; we worked nights and weekends from our apartments. It didn't take us long to realize how passionate we were about growing this idea into a successful business, and we knew that it would never last as a side gig. So we ceremoniously quit our jobs on the same day, handed in our two-week notice, and walked out of the corporate world together on May 4, 2012. Our lives haven't been the same since.

Networking has driven our business since day one. We also made it a top priority to spend time working on our own social media strategy. Our efforts quickly paid off but not without a lot of sweat, blood, and tweets. By the end of 2013, our company ranked on the first page of Google when consumers searched "social media agency." Because of this, we now get a ton of qualified leads through our website, all of which would not be possible without diligently following our own social media strategy. That's right—social media can be a very powerful search engine optimization (SEO) tactic!

Throughout this journey, we've met a lot of talented and motivated females to whom we owe much of our success. This book is our way of showing gratitude for our strong network of support and paying it forward to another group of strong female entrepreneurs. Ladies, you can become anything you want, and social media can help you get there!

STEPHANIE ABRAMS CARTIN

Even as a small child, my family knew I would be an entrepreneur. I grew up in Rockville, Maryland and at the age of five, I was selling lemonade, and at the age of ten, I had the hottest Beanie Baby resale business in Montgomery county. A couple of decades later, there is no place I'd rather be than running my own business. Let me give you a little background on how I went from lemonade and Beanie Babies to Facebook Ads and Google+.

I attended the Cornell University School of Hotel Administration and joined Facebook during my sophomore year. At that time, you had to have an Ivy League .edu e-mail address to join the community. I knew from the start that Facebook would change the future of marketing. After graduating in 2006, I went to work for Marriott Vacation Club in Orlando, Florida, where I quickly became a top salesperson.

In 2008 I was recruited by another hospitality company and moved to New York City. Sales and networking came second nature to me, but I was also intent on staying on top of the social media trends. I realized that there was a great need for small businesses to start using these platforms to grow their business and reach their customers. In 2009 I cofounded a social media agency called Gabbaroo. My partner eventually moved on to start a family, and I returned to a full-time sales position.

When I started looking for a new business partner, I was introduced to Courtney through Susie, a successful entrepreneur who had begun her company in college. I knew that Courtney and I shared a similar vision, passion, and drive to grow our ideas into a successful business. In 2011 we cofounded Collective Media, which is now Socialfly, and haven't looked back.

From the beginning of our journey as female business owners, we recognized how important our network of support was to our success. We developed the idea of a group of women who could share their wisdom, knowledge, and experience to help each other on their individual paths. In 2012 we cofounded Startups in Stilettos™, an exclusive female networking group. Throughout the year, we host events to bring together women running startups of all sizes in every industry imaginable. We're writing this book as an accessory to all you stiletto-wearing women who want to succeed in the business world.

Preface

en·tre·pre·nista

ˌäntrəprəˈnees-ˈta/

noun

1. A woman who organizes and operates a business or businesses, taking on greater than normal financial risks in order to do so. One who has a drive, passion, and vision, with an undying determination to succeed. She is fiercely motivated, ambitious, and competitive, forging her own path to independence and success.

We already know something about you simply based on the fact that you are reading this book. First, you've started your own business. This speaks to how driven and ambitious you are. Next, you are brave. Trying to build something from scratch, especially in the business world, can be a daunting and frightening journey. You also have a vision—your reason for starting a business—and are both passionate and resourceful. We've just summed up the basic and necessary attributes of all those who try to start and grow their own business. All of these traits will certainly be put to the test, if they haven't been already, time and time again.

One last thing we know about you is that you are smart—smart enough to be reading this book and smart enough to recognize that social media has become a *must* and that leveraging its power can be instrumental in taking your business to new levels. Even if you are in the infant stages of starting your own business, or if instead of being a founder, you are a leading businesswoman who works in a team at a startup, you can still benefit from reading the tips and tricks we are about to share in the chapters of this handy guide.

We'll give you a little background before we get started. We decided to write this book for many reasons. Primarily, it was because we once stood in your shoes. We were two females filled with big dreams, sprinkled with good ideas, and mixed with drive and self-belief. When we first decided to start our own business, we were, in retrospect, oblivious to all we were getting ourselves into. At the time, ignorance certainly was bliss, as we didn't know how much we actually didn't know. However, as we began to gain momentum and learn from our mistakes, we quickly recognized one important factor in our success: the help of our fellow entre-prenistas. We were amazed at the support we found through a network of women so open to sharing their knowledge and experience.

Listening and learning from others who had already blazed the trail ahead of us taught us more than we ever imagined possible. We learned more from these women than any class, seminar, or business coach could ever teach us. Without their help and guidance, we easily would have been lost. Now it is our turn to give back. We want to help. We want to see you and your business succeed. In order to get you there, we share some of the tricks, tools, and tips we have employed in successfully using social media to help our clients market their businesses.

Our baby, brainchild, and passion is our company, Socialfly. We are a social media marketing and public relations (PR) agency based in New York City, and we specialize in helping brands develop comprehensive social media marketing and PR strategies to generate leads, facilitate brand awareness, assist with reputation management, and drive sales. We create and execute a strategy on our clients' behalf by leveraging social media platforms such as Facebook, Twitter, Pinterest, Instagram, and Google+. Helping our clients grow their online crowd feels great, but helping them grow their bottom line feels even better.

Let's be real. When your tooth hurts, you go to a dentist. Why? A dentist is a professional with experience and expertise to help rid you of your pain. You started your business because you are great at what you do. You are the subject matter expert. If you've opened a hair salon, you are undoubtedly great with styling hair. If we need highlights or a blowout to look fabulous, we come to your salon. If you are a stylist, you know fashion like the back of your hand. When we're in desperate need of a wardrobe makeover, you're our new BFF. Knowing when to turn to a professional is smart.

Unfortunately, smart and resourceful entrepreneurs sometimes allow their pride and undying belief in themselves to lead to some shortsighted decisions that negatively impact their business. This can be especially true for a business owner who already uses social media in her personal life. Knowing how to post to Facebook, send a tweet, or create a board on Pinterest does not make someone a social media expert, particularly as it pertains to successfully leveraging these platforms for business and achieving tangible, measurable results.

Just as we didn't when we first started our business, you probably don't even know what it is you don't know. But that's why you're reading this book, right? Benefit from our knowledge by following this guide and putting your new knowledge into action geared toward success. You already have a great product or service. Now let's make social media work for your business!

Introduction

When we first started Socialfly, our goal was to help entrepreneurs and small business owners market their business through social media. Our initial pitches were met with a great deal of resistance and even more indifference. We'd say things such as "Facebook business page," "pins to drive traffic to your website," and "maintain a presence on Twitter," and be met with "Why?" "I just don't get it!" "It's a fad," and "You can't measure ROI." Times have certainly changed, and fortunately for us, so has the conversation. Social media is no longer a maybe. It has been cemented as a must in any competitive and thorough business marketing strategy. Social media has changed the way your customers and prospects communicate and has become absolutely crucial for online branding, reputation management, and customer loyalty. But as good business owners, we know it often comes down to dollar signs. The bottom line is social media drives sales.

Ask any business owners how they get referrals and incremental business, and they usually have the same answer: word of mouth. Well, think of social media as digital word of mouth—on three shots of espresso. Not too long ago, people who needed a recommendation for a particular product or service would pick up the phone and, one by one, reach out to those they trusted most, such as family and friends. This basic human interaction still occurs, but these days, it's happening differently. With a few keystrokes and a tap on your iPhone, people now access their entire personal network all at once. As a business owner, this should thrill you. We live in a world where a fabulous pair of shoes is only as fabulous as the number of "likes" they receive on Instagram. "Like" it or not, social media drives sales, and our pitch is no longer about whether or not to play the game; it's about how well you play it.

Beyond word of mouth, Google search rank is the second most common answer we hear when asking business owners how they find new business. But like a best-dressed list, where you rank makes all the difference. Organic listings receive 90% of clicks. Paid ads receive 10% of clicks. Less than 10% of people advance to Page 2. Appearing of the first page of search results is gold for your business.

Google Result Page Rank	Average Traffic Score
1	32.5%
2	17.6%
3	11.4%
4	8.1%
5	6.1%

Figure 0.1. The figure shows the average amount of total traffic on the first five pages of a Google search. As you can see, the first page receives over a third of all traffic for a particular search, making it that much more important to have your business rank well. *Source: Google: http://chitika.com/google-positioning-value*

You can go about getting a coveted high-ranking position in a couple of different ways. First, there are hordes of SEO firms out there that charge a premium to ensure that your business is at, or close to, the top of a Google search. This works great ... until you stop paying, when suddenly your brand may be banished to page five with little or no hope of a comeback. Our approach can be more cost effective, and while it requires some time and patience, the results are great. Social media can actually improve your search rank. In 2014, Google updated its algorithm to heavily weigh social media activity in determining where a business ranks in an organic search.

We at Socialfly can directly speak to the power of social SEO, based on our own experience. We have worked with several brands that have never paid for SEO yet rank in the top five on Google. Several of these businesses even rank ahead of larger competitors. Can you hear that? It's the sound of their phones ringing with potential clients. We attribute a good portion of this high Google ranking to the fact that these companies post content across multiple social platforms every day. It does take planning, time, and consistency, but over time, posts on social media will improve your Google search rank.

Great, so now that we're all on the same page (Google search or otherwise), we must warn you against thinking this endeavor is simple and straightforward. After all, we built our business because we know it's complicated and even more time consuming. It takes more than just posting on multiple platforms daily to fully reap the rewards of a social media presence. Separate from the discipline of consistent posting, as well as monitoring the social conversations about your brand, you'll need one very important ingredient in this recipe for success: a strategy. Without developing a strategic road map for social media marketing, you will be lost. Social media isn't as simple as rolling out of bed and asking one of your employees, "What should we post today?" Social media marketing differs from a personal account, where the only people you are trying to engage with are your immediate network of friends and family. Your business needs to have a rhyme and reason to the messages you are sharing online. While it will take some time, effort, and creative thinking, your social media strategy will become a guide to your business, leading you down a path of increased leads, greater brand awareness, and elevated financial returns.

CHAPTER 1

Your Social Media Strategy

The who, what, where, when, and why questions

The prospect of creating an effective social media strategy shouldn't freak you out. Start with answering the basic questions, and before you know it, you'll have a plan.

First, you need to answer the question of why. *Why* are you using social media for your business? What are your overall goals and business objectives? Is it for leads and sales? Are you looking for increased awareness of your service, product, or brand? Will social media be used to engage with your customers and clients to manage complaints and receive feedback on products or services? These are the questions that should guide your every post, every tweet, and every dollar spent on social media advertising.

Next, you need to identify your audience. *Whom* do you wish to target? Give this audience a face. What's the age range, socio-economic status, and location? What does your audience's lifestyle look like? Think about your audience's interests, the types of things normally purchased, and family structure. This will help you craft contests and promotions that are appealing to your niche market. Answering this question will also allow you to properly leverage targeted social media advertisements (but more about this later).

Figure out your target market: gender, age, geography, marital status, parental status, and income level. An example target would be engaged females, ages 21–45, who live in metropolitan areas.

Now go even further. What do those women like? They might like designer brands, Beyoncé, Uber, Bloomingdales, *50 Shades of Grey*, and so on. Listing out the interests of your target market will help you craft your content and your advertisements.

Once you have sufficiently answered the question of whom to target, you can address the next big strategy question: What will you say to them?

What topics, information, and questions will not only catch the eye of your audience members but also encourage them to engage in a dialogue? Here's where you need to get inside the head of your prospective customer. Let's say your target market includes brides-to-be. Your content must be geared toward things that brides-to-be care about, whether it's the hottest trends in wedding dress styles or the latest DIY centerpieces. Giving your audience useful information is a surefire way to grab their attention and hold onto it. We already know it can't all be a hard sell (see Figure 1.1). Rather, you have to reward people for liking and following you by providing them with useful, relevant, and intriguing content. Here's where a conversation calendar comes in handy. Develop a plan for the story you will tell on each platform. Will your page be a source for tips, a behind-the-scenes look into your company, a place to voice questions and concerns, or a combination of the three? In most instances, a mix of relevant content has the greatest success in building a loyal following and cohesive brand awareness.

Bari Jay
Published by Socialfly NY [?] · March 1 · @

Here are 17 wedding cakes that prove glitter is always a good idea! Which is your favorite? --> http://bzfd.it/1BngN3P

Community Post: 17 Wedding Cakes That Prove Glitter Is Always A Good Idea
All that glitters is not gold. Sometimes it's actually cake.
BUZZFEED.COM I BY EMMA LORD

Figure 1.1. Bari Jay is a bridesmaid dress line that shares useful wedding tips and interesting content to grab the attention of anyone who might be engaged now or in the future. People who like a post about wedding cakes on the Bari Jay's page might not be engaged now, but this is a subtle way to stay top of mind when it comes time for them to dress their bridesmaids.

After you decide on the story you want to tell, ask yourself where you will post this information. Which platforms make the most sense for your business? More than likely, to answer that question you need to know where members of your target audience spend most of their time (see Figure 1.2). In almost all cases, a Facebook business page is the place to start. If you're an e-commerce brand, then leap on over to Pinterest, where you'll find a fierce following of women with cash to spend. If your target market is on the younger side, then you better believe that they are on Instagram, hashtagging away at this very second. You need to be where your prospects are before you can tackle the next big questions: What platforms should you use? Who uses those platforms? What platforms are best for what industries?

Social Media Network	Demographic
Facebook	1.49 Billion monthly active users (Q3 2015). Users are 45% women and 55% men. 77% of America's adult females are on the site and 66% of adult males. 87% of adults 18–29 use FB.
Twitter	316 Million monthly active users (June 2015). 24% of adult men use Twitter vs. 21% of adult women. 37% of adults 18–29 use Twitter.
Instagram	300 Million monthly active users (July 2015). 29% of online females and 22% of online males use Instagram. 53% of adults 18–29 use Instagram.
Google +	2.2 billion Google accounts, but 300 million active Google+ users (May 2015). 73.7% of users are male. 26.3% of users are female.
LinkedIn	364 Million users (July 2015). 28% of online men and 27% of online women use LinkedIn. 31% of adults 30–49 use LinkedIn. 44% are Americans with income of $75,000 or more.
Pinterest	70 million users (July 2015). 42% of online women and 13% of online men use Pinterest. 34% of adults 18–29 use Pinterest.

Figure 1.2. Social Media Platform Cheat Sheet. *Source: Sprout Social.*

When will you share? Figuring out what times make the most sense for you to post is important. Just to keep you on your toes (or rather your tablet), optimal timing may be different for each platform. Look at what you are doing now and see where the engagement is. If midday works best for Facebook, schedule your posts in advance to go out right after lunch. If Twitter is getting more of a response in the evening, shift your tweets to later in the day. You can find statistics on optimal times for each platform. In general, Twitter sees the most engagement during the workday. Facebook is more popular outside busy commuting hours. It makes sense that most people aren't on Facebook on a Friday night around dinnertime. However, you must be sensitive to what works for your audience and schedule accordingly. This all boils down to a testing game. If you're posting similar types of content in the morning and in the evening, you can easily find out which posts get the most views and see the most engagement.

One final component of an effective strategy is a thorough analysis of the competition. When asked to perform this exercise, our clients often say, "I don't care what they are doing. I want to differentiate myself from them. I don't want to do what they do." But to outshine the competition, it's imperative to know what they're up to. Learn from the good *and* the bad of what they are doing. You may learn that a platform isn't right for you when you see a competitor's lack of engagement or following. Your analysis may show you that your competition's audience seems indifferent to the content that is shared. Or you may learn something about your audience that you never realized before, such as that they just adore cute puppy photos (by the way, this is pretty much true of all audiences). Finalize your strategy by outlining gaps and opportunities for your business to leverage. Here's a brief list of questions that should be included in your competitive analysis:

- ✓ What platforms is your competitor using?

- ✓ At which times is your competitor posting content and how often?

- ✓ What content is getting the most engagement?

- ✓ What level of engagement, if any, is your competitor seeing?

- ✓ How is your competitor leveraging this engagement?

- ✓ What type of contests and promotions is your competitor running?

- ✓ What do you think is working?

- ✓ What do you think isn't working?

Once you have identified these key themes and sized up the competition, you have a blueprint for your social media plan of attack. But, wait, don't stop there! Develop some benchmarks so that you can track your progress and change your approach and direction if you are falling short or progressing too slowly. It is important to keep in mind that you will need to do periodic temperature checks to make sure your online approach is still a healthy one. Do not wait until you have failed to meet your overall goals to throw in the towel and say social media didn't work for your business. If something isn't working, adjust the plan and try a different tactic. One of the most important things to remember in the world of social media is that results take time. With your strategy as a guide, though, you'll know where you are along the path of social media success.

Note: Be sure to create all of your social media accounts using one e-mail address. More importantly, make sure you personally have access to that e-mail address so that you never lose access to an account in the event of an employee leaving your company.

CHAPTER 2

Facebook and Facebook Advertising

Who uses it, why it matters, and a bunch of how-to logistics such as creating content, scheduling in advance, and the power of Facebook advertising

S imply stated, Facebook should be the hub of your online presence. With over 1 billion users and over 750 million daily users, it's safe to assume that a large portion of your target market (if not the majority) is using Facebook. While other platforms may allow you to better connect with your target market, a well-designed Facebook page should be like an extension of your website and a gateway to other channels. However, Facebook can do much more than act as a landing page for your company. Separate from the reputation management and brand awareness it provides, Facebook's ability to target new customers will be an invaluable asset. Facebook knows a lot about its users—mostly because everyone is offering information all the time. Beyond age, gender, and location, Facebook also knows the music, movies, products, and services a user likes. As a marketer, you have access to all of this information.

Back in the "mad men era," marketers would run print or TV ads and take the shotgun approach: blast out your message and see what it hits within your target market. Facebook does the same, but now you are aiming with the precision of a laser. Want to target 20-something females in close proximity to your salon? Target specific zip codes. Want to target athletes within that smaller population? Drill down further by identifying those who like physical activity, sports, and health and wellness. Want to target only women within those groups? Want to target only those who are ages 30 and older? Facebook's advertising platform allows you to do all of this and more (see Figure 2.1). Then there's the flip side where users are actively searching for your business. Facebook added a graph search function that allows users to search for restaurants, salons, and other businesses by using Facebook as a search engine. If your business isn't on Facebook, you just took yourself out of the running. Recognizing the power at your fingertips is the first part of this process. The next part is knowing how to harness that power!

Figure 2.1. Here's just a snapshot of some of the targeting that is available to you through Facebook Ads.

Creating content is where your social media footprint begins. It is important to remember the reverberation of your brand's messages on Facebook. When a friend likes or shares one of your posts, it will now appear in the news feeds of those they are friends with, multiplying your potential audience. When a friend of this friend then engages with your content, it multiplies again. This can go on exponentially; it's how things go viral overnight. However, the content of the message that you send out is important and makes all the difference between a viral sensation and a post with zero engagement. Consumers are bombarded by information every minute of every day. How can you stand out from the deluge of messaging? Give your audience members useful, informative, and relevant information that connects and resonates with them.

Your first instinct will probably be to showcase your product or service, and this is definitely one type of post that should be included in the plan. It *cannot* be the only type, however. Let's go over some examples to get you thinking.

Humans are visual creatures, so beautiful photos will always resonate best. Always be on the lookout for a compelling snapshot to illustrate a message, highlight a product, or give a face to your company. Share behind-the-scenes snapshots of your office life. If you run a small business where you are the face of the company, go ahead and show people where you spent your Fourth of July weekend. Don't just post about yourself, though. Ask questions! Get people involved about subjects that align with your brand. Where is everyone else spending their holiday weekend? Which runway looks are your fans loving from New York Fashion Week (#NYFW)? Which cocktail would they pair with your featured appetizer?

If you are in the wellness space, then healthy eating tips, links to articles about nutrition, and motivational fitness quotes ("fitspi-ration") are all good content. If you are in the fashion retailer world, give sneak peeks at upcoming designs and inspiration for new lines. We are not saying you should share all of your advice, tips, and tricks, but you want to establish yourself as an authority, and one of the easiest ways to do that is to provide access to edu-cational, expert, and insider information.

We know its all about business, but it could be beneficial to show how you like to have fun while getting the job done and pleasing clients. You still want to maintain the voice of your brand and a level of professionalism, but it's okay (and necessary) to show that you're human. Some of the posts that we see garnering the most engagement are photos of employees doing what they love to do. It puts names and faces behind everything your company does and allows people to feel they know your team beyond the products or services you offer.

Creating content around major holidays or even National Donut Day, is a great way to build engagement. You'd be surprised at how many people will like their hair salon for wishing them a happy Labor Day. These types of posts can allow you to connect with your audience on a different level. Facebook now has a hashtag search feature, so when it makes sense (such as for major trending topics, including the #WorldCup or #BlackFriday), add a hashtag to the end of your posts so that they can show up in a search.

Ideally, you want to share original content with your audience. The reality is that you may not always have time to generate this content—and that's just fine! Plenty of major brands repurpose and share content from other sites and sources. You can link to articles that reinforce the perception that you are current and paying attention to what is happening in your business. If you can, write your own mini blog post breaking down a bigger article or providing your own unique take on the topic. Or post a link to an article with a caption that is short and sweet. Ask a question about a news item you are sharing, and get feedback from your Facebook fans. Remember to give credit to the original creator of the content, and tag other brands whenever possible. Share the love; it really will come back to you.

We always recommend including a visual with every post. As we stated earlier and likely will again and again (our apologies for sounding like a broken record), beautiful, high-resolution, correctly sized photos are vital for the success of your content and advertising campaigns. We live in a day and age when people would rather see a picture than read. So make sure your pictures stand out from the crowd. Another emerging type of content on Facebook is videos. Facebook's algorithm favors video content. Have you noticed that videos sometimes play automatically as you are scrolling through your news feed? Well, this is another opportunity to stand out. All videos should be posted natively to Facebook. Simply posting a YouTube link will not get as much traction on Facebook as it used to (see Figure 2.2).

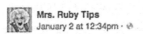

Mrs. Ruby Tips
January 2 at 12:34pm · 🌐

If you're anything like old Ruby here, you've packed on plenty of pounds over the holidays. Join me in starting 2015 off right. Watch my latest video below and learn how to make my marvelous Morning Glory Smoothie! You can grab the full recipe here. --> http://bit.ly/RTSmoothie

4,902 Views
Like · Comment · Share · 👍 92 💬 3 ↪ 59

Figure 2.2. In this example, the video has been uploaded straight to Facebook so it is easy for your Facebook fans to watch. You'll notice you can still add another link in the caption to drive people to your website or YouTube channel.

Now, before you start posting, refer back to your strategy. We want you to outline the types of posts you intend to use. At first, it's going to be time consuming to figure out what to post, how to post it, and how to be a pro at both. We suggest giving yourself several hours on the weekend or Monday to plan out your content. Depending on your business, it may make sense to plan out a week's worth of content at a time, or go ahead and plan out a full month if you are able to. Trying to remember to post something every day can be a challenge, leading to inconsistency in the timing and the content you share. It becomes a "What should I post today?" mentality. If you are posting simply because you remember that you should, you are already behind the eight ball. Put some time and thought into your approach, always referring back to your strategy and, ultimately, your objectives. By scheduling content in advance, your life will become a lot easier. So keep reading.

Things to post:

- ✓ holiday posts
- ✓ links to relevant articles
- ✓ behind the scenes
- ✓ press mentions
- ✓ questions
- ✓ quotes
- ✓ videos
- ✓ tips
- ✓ links to your blog
- ✓ offers/promotions
- ✓ showcase products and services

Next, we guide you through scheduling a post for a specific time and date on Facebook. We also detail how to include links and upload photos and videos.

STEP 1: Log into your Facebook page as an administrator. Look for the box in which you would normally type a post (status). Make sure you are "using the page as" your business and not you as a person.

You'll want to see your business's icon in the left hand corner, not your personal profile photo. This is how you'll know you are posting as the business itself.

STEP 2: Type what you would like to share. Are you including a link to a story or video? There are several sites that offer link shortening and tracking capabilities. Our personal favorite is the free link-shortening tool Bitly. It will shorten the link and provide click-through data so that you can see how many people took the time to actually open what you shared.

Although an image will automatically generate when you include a link, we still recommend uploading your own photo if the generated image doesn't appear large enough or doesn't showcase what the link is really about. After an image automatically generates, you can post your own photo, which will override the automatic image.

Once you put the link in the post box, you'll notice the **Upload Image** option, which is what you should do if the image that comes up isn't clear or doesn't highlight the section of the website where you are directing your fans. Above, the photo is clear and showcases the home page of www.socialflyny.com, so it's good to go.

STEP 3: There are two ways to add an image. You can click on Video/Photo, or you can click on the camera icon in the bottom right of the dialogue box. Make sure your photos are sized correctly for Facebook. This can be tricky because the sizes of images that appear in your news feed, on mobile, and on the timeline can differ. Generally, you want your pictures to be PNG files.

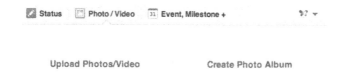

When you click on **Photo/Video,** you'll then have the option to upload photos or video to the post or to create an entire photo album.

STEP 4: Now that your copy is written with a shortened link or uploaded photo, click on the **Post** icon (lower right) to post immediately, or click the arrow to schedule. Facebook allows you to save it as a draft to be scheduled at a later time, or you can click on **Schedule**, which will then give you an option for a day and time. Note: you can schedule out up to six months in advance. You can also "backdate" a post, which will publish the post to your timeline with an old date, but it won't be pushed out live to a newsfeed audience.

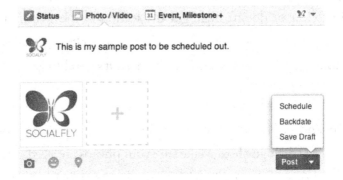

In this example, we hit the arrow so that we now have the option to schedule our post in advance.

Select the day and time you would like your post published. Once you have done so, click on **Schedule Post**. Facebook will alert you that your post has been scheduled and will prompt you to view the activity log.

Even if you don't do so immediately, you always have the option to go back and see everything scheduled. We recommend always looking at your posts before they go out. This gives you another chance to proofread, ensure the photo is presented properly, and test any links. You can view your scheduled posts any time by clicking on **Publishing Tools** in the header at the top and then clicking on **Scheduled Posts**.

Here you will see an activity log of all posts that have been published to the page as well as an option on the left to view scheduled posts and drafts.

When viewing posts in the activity log, you'll have the option to reschedule the post to a different time/date from what was originally planned, to edit the post's caption, or to delete the scheduled post entirely.

You'll only be able to see a handful of scheduled posts at a time, but you can schedule multiple months in advance. Click on **Show More**, below the last post shown, and more will appear.

So you've scheduled your content. Now what? Your job is not finished. There are two actions you must now take.

1. Facebook, being the public company that it now is, makes its money from advertising. In 2014, Facebook truly became a pay-to-play platform. Without a budget for promoting your

posts, a very small percentage (if any) of your fans will see your content. Strategically boosting all of your posts is key. You can boost your posts to your current fans and your exact target market. Your posts will then appear in the news feeds of the exact people you are trying to target. Boosting your posts does not require you to break the bank. A boosted post of $10 can go a long way, especially if your content is good. However, the more you spend, the more people you will reach. Stay tuned for our Facebook advertising section.

2. Community management is imperative. If your content strategy is spot on, your fans will like, comment, and share. Your fans want to be heard, and validating them by responding to their comments or liking their posts is key (see Figure 2.3). You cannot ignore your page for the rest of the month simply because you have content going out every day. If you have piqued someone's interest, your Facebook page now serves as an avenue through which they can reach out and communicate with you directly— and immediately! No phone number to call. No e-mail to send. They can comment right then and there. Better yet, your entire audience of fans can witness the interaction. Perhaps, they ask for some pricing. Maybe they have a question about what you offer. When you answer, *everyone* can see it. Believe it or not, this is even better when there is a problem. Someone is unhappy? Don't panic. Handle it well and you can turn a detractor into a brand advocate. And since everyone can clearly see how quickly you react to rectify the problem and how your business presented itself throughout the process, the reverberation of these interactions can be exponentially powerful for you.

These are so good, I by myself managed to polish off a bottle of champaign & had a tough time getting out if bed the next day... Well worth it!
Like · Reply · 👍 1 · December 29, 2014 at 4:13pm

> Mrs. Ruby Tips You sound like my kind of gal, Sharon. Consider it practice for tonight, gorgeous!
> Like · December 31, 2014 at 10:24am

Would LOVE to go to one of your soirée someday, it would be sooooooo much fun 😀
Like · Reply · 👍 1 · December 29, 2014 at 1:04pm

> Mrs. Ruby Tips Thank you, Beatriz! I'm sure your soirées are smashing, as well - especially if you include my cocktail recipes! 😊
> Like · December 29, 2014 at 1:18pm

She sure was a refreshing gal wasn't she !
Like · Reply · 👍 1 · December 30, 2014 at 8:47am · Edited

Write a comment...

Figure 2.3. This is an example of how you can respond to all of the people commenting on your photos.

Customers have so many options nowadays; these relationships should be seen as fragile. It's helpful to look at a Facebook page such as a page in the wonderful (or not so wonderful) world of dating. There is a discovery process. People have to get to know you and you have to get to know them—their passions, their likes, their dislikes, and, generally, what makes them tick. You don't pick them up for a date and move in for a kiss right away. Your job as a marketer is to woo your audience with your messaging. Offer some value before expecting prospective customers to give you their business. Most importantly, be ready to listen! Decipher which posts are performing the best, and infer which types of information your audience responds to. Reply to all comments, or simply like a comment to show that you saw it. Answer all questions. Engage with your audience. First impressions can make or break you. Remember this as you develop your strategy.

Now that you have content and a page worth visiting, it's imperative that you start running Facebook Ads. Facebook Ads are a great way to help grow your audience in terms of page likes, which give your business credibility on Facebook. When people like your page, they are essentially opting in to your marketing messages, and all of their friends will see that they liked you, giving you even more clout. They want to hear what your brand has to say and offer and, maybe, their friends do too. A simple "LIKE US if you like xyz" ad can, surprisingly, do wonders for how many people opt in to your Facebook content. The bigger the audience, the more opportunity there is for your business. Think of it as fishing. The bigger the net you cast, the more fish you are likely to catch. But the biggest net in the ocean is meaningless if you aren't casting it near the fish. This is where targeting comes into play. The Facebook targeting capabilities are tremendous. Likes are great, but if they aren't from someone genuinely interested in what you do, the added like is meaningless. You want an audience that will actively engage with your brand, which is why it's important to choose your target market carefully (see Figure 2.4).

Audience Definition

Your audience is defined.

Specific — Broad

Audience Details:
- Location:
  - United States
- Relationship Status:
  - Engaged
- Age:
  - 21 - 60
- Gender:
  - Female

Potential Reach: 2,200,000 people

Figure 2.4. This is an example of targeting. The selected audience is newly engaged females between the ages of 21 and 60, residing in the United States.

To run a Facebook Ad, first you need to decide on a budget. Facebook allows you to set a per-day budget or a lifetime budget.

Unlike when you tell yourself you'll only spend $100 on a shopping trip, Facebook stays true to the monetary guidelines you set. The company will not spend a cent over your set budget. You can spend as little as $5 per day or thousands of dollars per month. There is no limit.

Here's how to begin setting up your ads.

STEP 1: Click on the white arrow on the top right corner of your Facebook page. Select **Create Ads** from the drop-down menu.

STEP 2: You'll see several options as to what you hope to accomplish through the ads. We recommend beginning with **Promote Your Page** to get page likes. This will be the easiest way to quickly

grow your Facebook audience with the least amount of money. Down the line, you can play around with website ads and website conversions, but you want to be liked, right? Let's get you some fans.

STEP 3: Choose your targeting. Follow the prompts to narrow down an audience that is specific to your brand.

An ideal audience size is at least 500,000, but it really depends on your company. Choosing a small, highly targeted audience will, generally, mean that your ads will have a higher cost per like. However, if you have a restaurant in New York City, it makes sense that your audience will be much smaller than an online store seeking to target the entire country. Your audience should look like your potential customers.

STEP 4: Define your budget in the **Campaign and Ad Set** dialogue box. Name your campaign (something like "August LIKE ads" is all you need). Really committing to continuous advertising is important, so we recommend running a per-day budget. If you want to run a lifetime budget to test out a specific amount for one month, you can. Just be aware that starting and stopping the budget at the end/beginning of the month will give you some lag time instead of having continuously running ads. If you change the budget structure from lifetime to per day in the middle of the campaign, it can alter results. We recommend starting from scratch when you want to make these types of changes.

STEP 5: Decide whether you are bidding for likes, clicks, or impressions. Once again, we recommend sticking with the goal of obtaining likes to start, so select Optimize for Page Likes. In contrast, bidding for clicks will put most money into the ad that is receiving the most clicks, and bidding for *impressions* will put most money into the ad that is shown to most people. (An impression is a user who sees your ad.) You want your ads to be seen, to be clicked on, and subsequently, to render new fans (i.e., generate likes).

STEP 6: You'll be prompted to select up to six images to test. Click on the box where it says **Upload**, and select your desired image, or select **Browse Library** to search Facebook's free images, courtesy of Shutterstock. Here we recommend testing six different photos. Think about what will be the most appealing image to your audience, but be prepared that you might be wrong. Sometimes, the photo we think is the most engaging doesn't receive the best results. The photo is the most important part of the ad, though, so make sure you are choosing quality images to represent your brand.

STEP 7: Type your ad copy into the text box. You'll notice you have only 90 characters. The ad preview will show on your right, so you can see exactly how the copy will appear with the images.

If your image is getting cut off, you can reposition it by clicking on **Crop** under the image upload box.

Make your edits to the copy and the headline on the left side of the screen, and your ad preview will show up on the right. Make sure your images are positioned correctly before placing your ads.

There is a certain degree of science to running these ads and a great deal of trial, monitoring, and tweaking. First, you make a compelling call to action. Second, you select a sampling of images to see which are getting the best reaction and results. Third, you run tests to see which copy coupled with which image is getting the best response. A common mistake made by business owners is that they try one ad, and when it doesn't get much traction, they declare, "This doesn't work." There is a trial-and-error process you must go through, but Facebook will help out by automatically putting more money into the image that is performing the best within a given campaign. After the first couple of days, you'll notice that one or two photos have used the majority of the budget spent thus far. This tells you which images are resonating more with fans and receiving the most new likes on the page. Before you get too excited about Facebook willing to help you out like that, make sure you read through this entire section to understand what role you play in monitoring and adjusting your ads.

STEP 8: Decide where your ads will run. Facebook runs ads in a user's actual news feed. You probably see these types of ads all the time whether you notice them or not. They appear marked with a tiny "Sponsored" at the top of what looks like a normal post. You can also run ads in the right column of the news feed, and mobile ads are available as well. We recommend clicking on **Remove** on the right-hand column ads. An ad in the news feed looks more like content than other placements and will, typically, see the most success. However, test these ads for yourself and see which deliver the best results based on your goals.

You choose your ad placement in the same space where the ad preview is shown. Clicking on **Remove** will take this type of ad placement out of your campaign. Otherwise, Facebook will test out all three types. In the screenshot above, the right column ads have been removed, which is why you see the **Add** option to add them back in.

STEP 9: Review your order. Look back over everything, and make sure there are no typos and that your photos appear how you want them to look in someone's news feed. Now you're ready to place your order. Facebook will alert you that your ads are being reviewed. Facebook looks at each and every ad to make sure there is no inappropriate content. Certain businesses and messaging will be banned to users under the age of 18, for example. Once your ads get approved (this usually takes less than 24 hours), they will start running. Congratulations, you are advertising on Facebook!

What's next? Don't forget about those ads! Monitoring your campaign needs to be a part of your daily schedule. To monitor your ads, hit that top right arrow on your home news feed or on the page and click on **Manage Ads.**

HOW TO MONITOR

Once you're in Ads Manager, you should see all of the campaigns you are currently running as well as old campaigns. Clicking a campaign will pull up the individual ads (each photo). Here is where you will see a lot of numbers, but don't get overwhelmed. You should focus on "Reach," "Impressions," "Engagement," and "Cost" to start. Your cost-per-like number is important to watch. This tells you how much you are spending for each new like on the page. There is no hard and fast rule about what this number will be; it varies by industry. However, in general, anything under $1.00 per like is considered good. Your cost per like will vary depending on the audience you are targeting. Generally, a younger audience will cost less per like. The success of an ad is highly dependent on the picture associated with the ad and the audience you are targeting. When advertising for the first time, we always recommend testing different audiences to get a sense of what each segment will cost you in terms of cost per like.

It's very important to let your ads run for at least a week before making any changes. After a week has gone by, you can pause any ads that aren't performing well or decide to tweak your target market or ad copy. It's a good idea to look over the other numbers in the row. "Reach" is an estimate of the number of people your ad is being shown to. "Frequency" is the average number of times an ad is served to one person. "Clicks" is how many people actually clicked on the ad, and "Results" is how many people actually liked that ad (simply stated, your new fans).

Once a campaign is running, you'll notice small fluctuations in cost per like. Make sure you are checking your campaigns at least once a week. If the cost per like ever jumps up, you'll know it is time to create new ads. It's good to change ads at least seasonally, and it's always important to be aware of major holidays, shopping seasons, and world events. It is likely that during the holiday season, ads will be more expensive, as you will be competing with many brands to get your messaging seen. This is why you should have a year-round Facebook strategy!

Once you have an audience, it's important to continue spending money on Facebook advertising so that your page never goes stagnant. As mentioned earlier, you'll also want to allocate a certain portion of your budget into boosting posts.

BOOSTING POSTS

In order to get your posts seen, Facebook has made it necessary to put money into a post. Under the status box, you may have noticed a **Boost Post** option. This is a way to spend a few dollars to expand the audience viewing your post. Recent changes to Facebook have lowered the organic reach of business posts. Unless you already have a massive following of fans that have liked your page, it may be disappointing to see that your post has only reached a small audience. Make sure you are boosting anything that is specifically driving traffic to your website or announcing a promotion. If you have 50,000 fans but your promotion is only being shown to 300 people, you aren't capitalizing on your powerful audience. Boosting your post is an inexpensive way to greatly increase your reach. When you go to boost a post, you'll have the option of targeting current fans or a new audience. Play around with what makes sense. You have the power to target your specific target audience. Be strategic about which posts you boost.

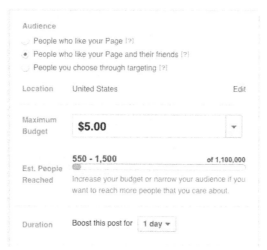

Figure 2.5. You'll notice in the screenshot above you can target only the fans of your page or expand the reach to friends of your fans. You can also select an entire new target market altogether.

FACEBOOK OFFERS

Running a Facebook offer is another easy way for you to see what your social media marketing spend is delivering. This is a quick and easy way to measure ROI. How many people claimed the offer and bought the product or service? How much did you spend promoting the offer? When you go to post on the page, you'll see an option for running an offer or creating an event. Offers are, typically, meant for businesses with brick-and-mortar shops, but online retailers can also take advantage of this platform. Simply figure out what deal or percentage discount you would like to offer and set it up to run directly on your page. Each person who claims the offer will receive an e-mail with the specific coupon code to shop on your site or the voucher to redeem in-store.

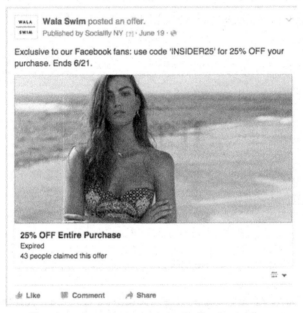

The above image is an example of a Facebook offer.

OTHER ADS

Aside from increasing your page likes and boosting your posts, you can also focus your ads on driving traffic to your website, increasing website conversions, or increasing video views or app downloads. The logistics of how to set up these ads are very similar to what we have already discussed: visuals, copy, and your target audience are key.

However, in website or conversion ads, you can add call-to-action buttons such as **Shop Now, Learn More,** or **Download Now.** These call-to-action buttons can be vital in getting someone to click on your desired link. Facebook has also developed standard website advertisements to include a conversion pixel. This pixel can measure certain actions that might be hard to see in Google Analytics. If you aren't familiar with Google Analytics, whoever set up your website should be able to help you. Google Analytics shows how traffic is coming to your website and also tracks sales. However, Google Analytics is limited in the extent to which it can measure social purchases, so this is where the conversion pixel comes in. The most common question that we get from our clients is "How can we measure ROI?" While the conversion pixel does not measure the true extent of ROI, it can measure how many clicks from the Facebook ad resulted in a purchase. This conversion pixel can measure how many people clicked on the ad and then came back at some point over the next few weeks.

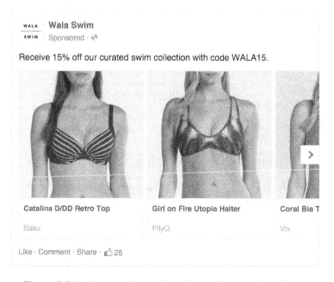

Figure 2.6. In this website ad, there is an offer code that allows the company to track ROI from this particular sale.

Figure 2.7. In this website ad, while there is no coupon code, if the business has a conversion pixel set up, it will be able to track how many people clicked on this ad and then made a purchase on the website.

All of this may seem daunting, but remember that a little money on Facebook goes a long way. Compare this to how much it costs to advertise in print or on television. Use the audience that is at your fingertips and stay within your budget. Just $5 a day can make a huge impact.

#Dothis

- ✓ Post content that is boosted to ensure that people see your posts.

- ✓ Engage with someone when they like, comment, or share.

- ✓ Include images in your posts.

- ✓ Offer a variety of information useful to your target demographic.

- ✓ Include a hashtag so that your content can be found by someone searching a topic.

- ✓ Honor and celebrate holidays.

- ✓ Continually advertise.

- ✓ Strategically boost posts.

- ✓ Run an offer.

- ✓ Add Facebook page name to windows, business cards, vehicles, and all marketing materials.

@Absolutely don't

- ✗ include more than one hashtag;

- ✗ be overly sales-y with every single post;

- ✗ write paragraphs with every post; and

- ✗ spend hundreds of dollars on advertising without monitoring the ads.

CASE STUDY

We love Facebook. Facebook can do wonders for your business if a proper strategy is in place. We have helped hundreds of businesses over the years capitalize on the tools available within Facebook to expand their reach and attract their current and new customers. One of our favorite case studies comes from one of our first Socialfly clients. A Made in the USA handbag and accessories line approached us to create and manage the company's social media strategy. Being instant fans of this company's products made our challenge even easier. The female founder of this company immediately explained to us the following challenges:

- ✓ She wanted to develop a voice and personality behind the brand.

- ✓ She wanted to increase her fan base to be able to compete with her large competitors.

- ✓ She wanted her fans to feel appreciated and loved.

- ✓ She wanted her fans' feedback on new styles and patterns.

We knew that Facebook would be the perfect place for her to achieve these goals, so we immediately went to work researching what her competitors were doing and what her target market was interested in. We developed a brand voice. We spent hours working with the client to create content, advertisements, and campaigns that would make her stand out from her competitors. Within two weeks, we had crafted a strategy and plan of attack that included:

- Making this dynamic female founder the focal point of the posts. This included posts of her adorable kids and behind-the-scenes shots of photo shoots and events.

- We leveraged her lifestyle photo shoots to create compelling "like" advertisements, targeting people who like her competitors on Facebook. We wanted to get her current fans to like her page on Facebook, so we imported her impressive mailing list into Facebook and targeted them with ads. Once that list was exhausted, we used Facebook tools to create a look-alike audience (an audience that has characteristics or interests similar to people on her e-mail list). We then created ads targeting her look-alike audience and got her cost-per-like down to 20 cents.

- We made her fans feel appreciated. We were diligent about responding to every single comment on the page. Our content included questions that would get people talking. We wanted everyone to feel heard; we also wanted everyone to feel loved. Every month we hosted a giveaway on our client's Facebook page, offering signature items from her line.

THE OUTCOME

- **1,349%** increase in Facebook audience
- **2,000+** e-mail addresses collected during seasonal campaigns

THE MORAL OF THE STORY

Once we created an engaged audience, we were able to tap into audience members for advice and feedback on new styles and patterns for future collections. Fans felt that they were a part of the design process and were eager to give their feedback. The brand was able to easily create products and new designs that it knew would be a hit.

Achieving this level of success on Facebook takes time and a disciplined strategy. Over time, we knew exactly the types of posts that would resonate with fans and get people talking. With a little creativity, dedication, and persistence, you can achieve these results as well. You go, girls!

CHAPTER 3

Twitter

All the basics again, such as who uses it, why it matters, and some how-to logistics including scheduling tweets and maximizing efforts

Twitter is often the platform our clients are the most confused about. It is a platform that has evolved tremendously since it first started and is evolving even as we write these words. If you have been a Twitter user for the past few years, you will have noticed that in 2014 something interesting happened. Its appearance changed drastically and yet looked strangely familiar. I can only imagine Facebook's reaction in seeing its archenemy enter the scene wearing the same dress! Yes, Twitter looks a lot like Facebook these days. But don't confuse the two; they are still drastically different. Yes, Twitter has evolved beyond its short-form text roots to include other media, such as pictures and videos, and has even added a new marketing tool called the Twitter Card. Much as we did with Facebook, with Twitter's IPO, we have seen drastic changes come to market. These current changes and future ones will provide more opportunities for marketers. Currently, Twitter is a great place to establish your brand voice, provide quick customer service, build relationships with current customers, start relationships with potential new ones, and even gain media attention. In this chapter, we show you some quick and easy tactics to help you stand out from the crowd, both personally and professionally.

We often tell clients to view Twitter as a branding tool. It is another place to circulate engaging content relevant to your audience and to participate in existing conversations. Think of Twitter as a digital cocktail party where you have the opportunity to mix and mingle every day (ahh, the perfect platform for all of the social butterflies reading this). People use Twitter for a variety of reasons, but some of the more common ones include news, keeping tabs on a favorite celebrity or entertainment personality, and customer service with brands. Unlike Facebook, most posts are public; people who are posting want to be heard and want you to talk to them. The best way to do this is to search for specific key words. For example, if you are working in real estate, do a search for people talking about moving or looking for an apartment in New York City. These tweets do exist, and the people talking about this topic are gold for real estate agents.

Growing a following on Twitter can be a much slower process than on Facebook, especially because Twitter's advertising platform is not as robust and, typically, much more expensive. So how can you attract a following without spending thousands of dollars? Think of how you would attract people to talk to at a cocktail party. Be interesting. Be funny. Be provocative. Have an opinion. It is important to have a personality on Twitter, which is a difficult task for many businesses. What's most important, though, on Twitter, is having a presence and consistent voice. Let people know that you are there and that you are active, and the followers will eventually come. Go beyond just that and start conversations with strangers, bloggers, and even media outlets. Get their attention by talking about what they are tweeting about. Pay attention!

Figure 3.1. Here's an example of a brand engaging with someone on Twitter. It's not overtly promotional, but it's a way to grab a prospective customer's attention.

One of the best ways to get attention on Twitter is to tap into trending hashtags. For those of you who don't know, a hashtag is a key word that categorizes the topic you are talking about. Twitter started the hashtag trend, and other platforms took notice. To capitalize on hashtags, you should always follow what is trending. Often, trending topics are about world news, TV shows, award shows, celebrities, scandals, and major sporting events. As we write this, a new season of *The Bachelor* is premiering on ABC. If your audience members are the type of people who watch that show, now is an excellent opportunity to tweet about the show and somehow relate it back to your company. It might also benefit you to search what people are saying about the show and try to start conversations. The brands or personalities that are witty and not shy are the accounts that win on Twitter. Twitter is a game that everyone can win.

As we mentioned earlier, Twitter is an excellent customer service tool. We are constantly searching Twitter to see what people are saying about our clients, and we always make sure to engage with those who are talking. It is most important to be responsive. People are always impressed with a prompt reply. In fact, a quick response is expected.

The ability for someone to communicate directly with your brand for information and obtain a resolution is undeniably powerful. Rather than calling an 800 number to fight with an automated operator, customers can now be direct and specific in detailing their problems ... and in singing their praises. In today's world, when someone is really happy with an experience, they often jump to social media to share. Let them share with their Twitter followers that they just bought the cutest purse from your store or had the best cheesecake ever or had a most pleasant experience with your service department. This is where it's imperative that you are on Twitter—listening and responding. If customers aren't happy, they *will* be tweeting about you. Give yourself an ear in the Twitterverse to listen and hear their concerns and, more importantly, manage your reputation (see Figures 3.2 and 3.3).

Figure 3.2. This is a great example of a customer testimonial on Twitter followed by a prompt response. You can turn a happy customer into a loyal fan and potentially a brand advocate for many more years to come.

Figure 3.3. In this example, the brand is Retweeting a positive comment from a fan.

Now that you know what to do, let's talk about how. First things first: How do you tweet? Once you set up a Twitter account (very basic on Twitter.com), you'll want to upload a profile picture (most likely your logo, but if you are using Twitter to build your personal brand, use a great, personable picture of yourself), a header image, and your bio. Your Twitter bio is a 160-character teaser to get people to opt in to your tweets. Show personality, grab people's attention, and most importantly, accurately depict your character or brand. Then you'll be ready to start tweeting. You'll notice that in composing a tweet, you are limited to 140 characters. So concision isn't just a suggestion; it's a must. This is where that link shortener, Bitly, is really important if you want to share an article or link to an item on your website.

Twitter is predominantly used on mobile, so you'll also want to download the free app to your phone. This makes managing mentions (anytime someone directly uses your Twitter handle to talk to or about you) extremely easy, as you will get notifications on your phone allowing you to respond right away to any questions or concerns. Depending on the size of your company and the popularity of your Twitter account, this may eventually become overwhelming. However, we recommend starting out by getting these notifications so that you can see who is interacting with you in real time.

There are other benefits to having Twitter on your phone, such as real-time live tweeting. If you are attending a major event (relevant to your business), it's good to engage with the brand involved and offer live commentary on what's going on. This gives your fans insight into an event that they couldn't go to or were not invited to. You have exclusive access and therefore exclusive content. Be a brand that shares inside information.

What should you share as content? It is often very easy to repurpose and reformat a Facebook post for Twitter. Share an article, but use fewer words. Find quotes that fit the character limit. Announce sales and promotions. Tweet relevant articles and blog links.

The next question regards when to tweet. Studies show that people use Twitter during the workday and that more links are read earlier in the week. Look at your own use—think about when you are on your phone and are most likely to read an article. Here's an example of how you can use timing to your advantage. Let's say your audience is *The Bachelor*-watching kind. Join in on the conversation! At the very least, schedule a tweet for that evening, saying you are gearing up to watch. Don't tweet a link to your blog that has nothing to do with the rose ceremony during that coveted time slot. Know your Twitter followers and schedule content accordingly. Brands that are witty and show a playful personality are the popular girls at the party.

Finally, find a way to start conversations with people. By "mentioning" someone in a tweet ("@Socialfly," for example), you are now directly engaging with that account. If you tweet someone and specifically mean to be conversational, then go ahead and start the tweet with the mention. This will show up in that person's feed and the feed of anyone following both of your accounts. However, if you want the tweet to be seen by all of your followers, put a period before the mention, or simply don't begin the tweet with that account's handle. If you want to attract the attention of bloggers, Twitter is the perfect place for you. Tweeting to bloggers and offering them a free trial of your app or a complimentary product is a great way to grab their attention and start building a lasting relationship with a potential future brand advocate. Use Twitter for your own PR. We worked with a brow salon in New York City and often invited beauty bloggers in for free treatments via Twitter. This tactic worked beautifully; not only did the bloggers receive beautifully plucked brows, but the salon received a glowing review. A true win-win.

Figure 3.4. It's always great to tweet directly to influencers who have used your product or service to prompt a testimonial or reply.

Figure 3.5. In this example, the brand reached out to a celebrity in the hopes of prompting a response. Even if Kelly Ripa doesn't respond, it's a good way to draw attention to a celebrity customer.

Now you have all these thoughts (in 140 characters or less), but who is actually going to see them? Growing your Twitter following is something that requires time and persistence. While there is the option for advertising on Twitter, in most cases this tends to be expensive and less strategic. Our advice is to save your advertising budget for Facebook and to grow your Twitter followers the organic way. One of the quickest ways to grow your following is to, first, be a follower. You will want to follow individuals, companies, and organizations that are considered leaders and authorities in your industry. If you own a nail salon, follow the major nail polish brands. If you own a hair salon, follow the major manufacturers of hair products. Follow style and fashion bloggers. Remember, engagement on social is everything, so be sure to be active. Retweet from these sources. Drill down even further and look at those who are following the experts in your industry. If you have a yoga studio, follow the big yoga apparel manufacturers. From there, drill down and look at who is following a brand such as @lululemon. Take a look at their profile. Chances are they are a prospect for you as well. Following your competition's followers is a great way to get followers for yourself. Every time you follow an account, that individual gets an e-mail notification. At the very least, those individuals are seeing your company and its profile flash across their screen. A lot of times, people will follow back.

Let your followers get to know you as you get to know them. Connect rather than solicit. In time, when the right bond is formed, it can and will happen naturally. Listening to what your likely customers like, want, and discuss can allow you to develop content that can be useful to them, thus proving your worth. Look at what's trending (see Figure 3.6). Twitter tells you what is being talked about every minute of every day. If you are viewing your Twitter feed on a desktop computer, you'll see "What's trending" on the left-hand side. Join the conversation when relevant and appropriate. Using the right hashtag can quickly multiply how many people see your message. Users will search by hashtag and then monitor the conversation and get involved. Being a part of it provides you another opportunity to reach and connect with your target audience.

The Internet and social media have made up-to-the-minute news a thing of the past. Information is now shared within seconds of an occurrence. Twitter breaks news

Trends · Change

#NationalUnderwearDay
National Underwear Day 2015: Celebrate With Celebrities In Their...
Just started trending

#LiteraryCakes
30 Gorgeous and Delicious Literary Cakes
Just started trending

#HarryBeCareful
367K Tweets about this trend

Lenny Kravitz
Lenny Kravitz rips trousers, accidently shows his manhood
158K Tweets about this trend

#FindMyStyleOnSnapdeal
14.7K Tweets about this trend

Joe Jackson
Joe Jackson leaves Brazil hospital after suffering stroke, 3 heart...
Just started trending

#AskTheWorldAQuestion
Just started trending

Colts
'We didn't' tip off Colts, Ravens say in statement
21.1K Tweets about this trend

Tim Blanks
Tim Blanks Joins the Industry Website The Business of Fashion
445 Tweets about this trend

Anjem Choudary
UK Charges Radical Islamic Cleric Anjem Choudary With 'Inviting...
13.3K Tweets about this trend

Figure 3.6. This is an example of trending topics. In some cases, a hashtag is being used. In other cases, the topic is just being discussed in general.

and stories before traditional news outlets. This allows you to stay abreast of what is really going on, especially what is specific to your industry's world. The ability to react and comment as things happen has changed the game. Keeping your finger on this pulse can provide great opportunities for engagement.

Next, we want to introduce you to a scheduling tool. We recommend using a management tool such as Hootsuite to schedule Twitter content in advance and to monitor conversations about your business. A basic Hootsuite account, at Hootsuite. com, is free and easy to set up. Hootsuite gives you a tour once you register, walking you through the basics. You can schedule tweets weeks in advance, similar to how you schedule your Facebook content. It's also much easier to see all mentions, direct messages, and sent tweets in one place. Hootsuite's search function can prove even more helpful. Click on the magnifying glass and search for any key words, and then click the locator button, allowing Hootsuite to access your location. Let's say you live in New York City, as we do. We can search for everyone talking about social media in NYC. Maybe some people are asking for help! Perhaps we'll start a conversation with them or follow them to catch their eye.

#Dothis

- ✓ Tweet frequently (multiple times a day).
- ✓ Retweet from key influencers.
- ✓ Follow industry leaders and professional organizations.
- ✓ Favorite relevant tweets from key influencers.
- ✓ Include a hashtag (or two).

- ✓ Respond, retweet, or favorite all mentions.
- ✓ Add your Twitter handle to business cards and all marketing materials.
- ✓ Link your e-mail to Twitter to import your contact list and grow your following.
- ✓ Participate in conversations relevant to your business.
- ✓ Use quotes.
- ✓ Use Twitter for customer service and respond in a timely manner.
- ✓ Tweet to bloggers and influencers to attract attention.
- ✓ Follow followers of your competition.
- ✓ Start conversations.
- ✓ Keep it short.
- ✓ Be authentic.
- ✓ Give clicks context.
- ✓ Make it visual—use photos!
- ✓ Know your audience.

@Absolutely don't

- ✗ include more than three hashtags;
- ✗ be overly sales-y;
- ✗ exceed the 140-character limit or your message will get cut off;

× send automatic direct messages (DM) to everyone who follows you (it looks like spam);

× give a play-by-play of your day (there is such a thing as oversharing on Twitter);

× connect your Twitter feed with Facebook—from a formatting perspective, it does not look good and can really turn off your Facebook fans; and

× mix personal with business, because while it can be good to share some personality and insight into your life outside work, your business account is not the place to voice political opinions or share frequent photos of your bachelorette parties.

CASE STUDY

Representatives of a brand-new denim company approached us. They were desperate for a solution to their number-one problem: their brand was unknown and had a small marketing budget. The denim market is a very competitive industry in the United States, so launching a brand-new denim line in a highly saturated market with a limited marketing budget is not an easy task. We quickly went to work researching their competitors and understanding what made their brand unique. Their denim was high quality at an affordable price. They were also redefining the market for moms' jeans. Their target market was trendy moms who wanted high-quality, forgiving jeans.

What does a company do when it wants to make a splash with a limited budget? Turn to Twitter! We quickly went to work and employed these tactics:

- We developed a fun tone and voice for the brand on Twitter.

- We wanted to attract moms and inspire them, so part of our content strategy was to tweet inspirational quotes.

- We tweeted to influencers, including celebrity moms, mommy bloggers, and media outlets.

THE OUTCOME

- Nina Garcia (who has over 1.9 million followers) retweeted one of our tweets to her fans, and suddenly, a tweet from our unknown jeans brand got over 23 retweets and 30 favorites—more retweets than the brand even had fans at the time. The tweet was a quote from Garcia that we related back to the brand.

- We tweeted to top mommy bloggers and offered to gift them complimentary jeans. This resulted in many tweets and gifts to bloggers who then wrote reviews and tweeted pictures of themselves in the jeans.

THE MORAL OF THE STORY

Strategically tweeting and starting conversations with bloggers can result in a larger reach than you ever dreamed of. And the best part is, all you have to do is identify the people at the Twitter party you want to talk to, walk up, and say hello!

CHAPTER 4

Instagram

What to post, how to grow a following, and how to leverage influencers

Instagram is a fast-growing visual social network. These days, most people with a smartphone have an Instagram account. While the user base is slightly younger than the overall Facebook audience, *some very powerful and lucrative demographics* are posting photos and following brands. If you are looking for a way to put a face to your company name, download the Instagram app immediately.

To help you decide if Instagram is the platform for you, below are some common goals it can help you achieve:

- interact with members of your target market and give them access to visual content
- attract new customers and build relationships with current customers
- raise brand awareness
- recruit employees
- encourage user-generated content (UGC)

When setting up your Instagram profile, keep a few things in mind. You'll want your Instagram handle to be the same as your Twitter handle if possible. This makes it easier for people to tag you on both. Also, be sure your settings are set to public so that people can see your photos and follow you without having to request your permission. You're a business; you don't want to turn anyone away! Also, make sure to include a link to your website in your bio, along with a short description of your company. This is the only area on Instagram that is clickable, one of Instagram's many marketing limitations. Instagram was not created for marketers. Recently, though, very large brands have sponsored posts, a marketing tool limited to brands with large marketing budgets. Don't let this new feature deter you. Instagram still remains a very cost-effective way to showcase your personality and brand through beautiful imagery, and by using the tactics in this chapter, you can conquer the platform with ease.

Instagram is all about image. Since it is photo based, taking and choosing eye-catching, stylistic images is crucial for your post and brand to get any love. Don't be intimidated, though, because Instagram is a fun and easy way to showcase your company's personality and build a loyal following. Behind-the-scenes photos of your employees hard at work and otherwise showcasing your company culture (see Figure 4.1) can also be a great recruiting tactic, ladies!

Figure 4.1. This is a behind-the-scenes look at the Socialfly office. It shows personality while also highlighting a new client.

Instagram is terrific for fashion, beauty, and food brands. If you have a visual product, this is one platform that you are going to want to devote some serious time to. You can showcase your products, flaunt your style, and demonstrate expertise (see Figure 4.2). Quality photos tell a powerful story, which is something to keep in mind when you think about who will have control over your Instagram account.

Figure 4.2. Beauty brands can find a way to promote their product as well as a lifestyle with visually appealing product shots.

So what should you post? The possibilities are endless, but scenery, cityscapes, food, puppies, babies, and quotes (in pretty fonts) tend to do well. Use this forum to be inspirational and informational. This isn't the place to be sales-y. Feature your product in picturesque settings. Show videos of your product in use (you are limited to 15 seconds). Give a peek into office life or build a lifestyle brand by featuring the types of food you eat, the places you travel, and the everyday finds that impress you. Did you walk by the most gorgeous window display this morning? Your followers want to see! If you are a fashion brand, your content should be a mix of the lifestyle of your brand, editorial images, and behind-the-scenes photos.

Posting on Instagram is simple. From within the app itself, you can post a photo or video in real time. You also have the option to choose any photo from your phone's library. Have members of your team text photos to whoever is in charge of Instagram for more diversity in your content. Did you find something cool online that you want to post? E-mail the photo to yourself, and save it on your phone. There is no way to schedule Instagram content, so this is one platform that you'll need to commit to being active on daily. Make sure to type in a short caption with your photo and include hashtags! Particularly on Instagram, this is how people will discover your brand. Of all the social media platforms, hashtags are, arguably, most important on Instagram. You can add as many hashtags as you want; just make sure they are relevant. The top hashtags are always changing, but #Food, #Love, #tbt, #latergram, and #Nofilter are always big ones. If you want to see just how these hashtags work, try searching for a major event such as New York Fashion Week (#NYFW or #NYFW15), and you'll be directed to countless photos (see Figure 4.3).

#nyfw

1,824,253 posts

TOP POSTS

Figure 4.3

You'll also notice the ability to simultaneously post to other platforms when you upload a photo to Instagram. Sometimes it's good to share your Instagram photos on your Facebook page, but be strategic and only do this occasionally. We are big fans of cross-promoting platforms, and this is a great way to do this.

Just as with Twitter, a great way to grow your following on Instagram is to follow others. Follow individuals who are good prospects. Read their bio. Do they fit your target market? If so, follow them, like their photos, and comment. One of our favorite tactics is to follow the followers of competitors. These users are clearly interested in the type of content that you will be posting. It's also good to be liked, so make sure you are searching and liking other people's photos. They'll get notified, see your business and profile, and may even opt in and follow you back. A quick word of advice: you are limited to how many people you can follow per day. Instagram does this to combat bots and click farms that mass-like. Be careful not to exceed the limit or you will get locked out of Instagram for several hours and will not be allowed to comment, like, or follow anyone.

Remember, as on Facebook and Twitter, it's very important to listen to the conversation. Search for hashtags involving your company name. People may be talking about you and not tagging you. Our clients who are new to Instagram are often surprised by how many people are posting pictures of their products, wearing their clothing, or eating at their restaurant. Instagram users love to document their everyday life, so don't be surprised if your brand is a topic of conversation. This type of post has many benefits: (1) you can repurpose this content by regramming it (through the use of third party apps) on other social networks or even Instagram; (2) you can comment back and build a lasting relationship with that customer; and (3) word of mouth (or visual impact, in this case) will extend beyond just those who follow you on Instagram.

Another important tactic on Instagram is searching for relevant hashtags. For example, if you are bringing a new health and wellness product to market, you will want to search hashtags such as #health, #wellness, #fitness, #eatwell, or #goodeats. These hashtags will give you great insight into what members of your target market are doing in their daily lives. What are they eating? What are they wearing? Are they exercising? People love to document their lives, and by commenting on, or liking, these photos you can grab the attention of the exact people you want to reach. This is a great way to get discovered and, eventually, liked, loved, and followed!

As on all social networks, people on Instagram love to talk, comment, and ask questions. This will likely happen when you start posting great content. So monitor your comments carefully. Sometimes, people will comment on old photos that you posted weeks ago, and those comments could fall through the cracks. Make sure you are responding to all questions and engaging with all mentions.

Involving your current fans and customers is another great tactic. Challenge them to share their pics of themselves in your place of business or using your products. Make it fun for you and for them. When asking your audience to do this, make sure you also ask that they use a special hashtag that is unique to your business. This will enable you to better discover content about your brand. We often recommend that our clients host photo contests. This type of contest helps raise brand awareness and also provides photo content to be repurposed. When utilizing this type of contest for your brand, we recommend that you offer an exciting and enticing prize, as this form of entry requires many steps. If you are managing an Instagram account with a large following, you will want to use social media contest software such as Woobox or Offerpop. We personally recommend Woobox, as it is very cost effective and will help you easily manage all contest entries by consolidating and counting all of the posts with a specific hashtag.

As we mentioned before, from a marketer's perspective, Instagram is not the easiest platform to use. Posts cannot be scheduled in advance, and as of the time of writing this, it is difficult even to see how many followers you have after you reach your first 10,000. There is software that you can use to find out how many followers you have, what your most liked pictures are, what filters get the most likes, and who likes your photos the most. One free software program that we recommend is Inconosquare. com. Another Instagram management site that we recommend is Crowdfire. This site will enable you to find out who is not following you back and will allow you to easily unfollow.

INFLUENCER OUTREACH

One of the best ways to grow your following and raise brand awareness is to get other users to post about you. This exposes your brand to the followers of the people who posted—and it gives you more credibility, because someone else is validating your product, location, or service. We find that this approach is easiest for clients in the hospitality industry, since people can tag their location on Instagram. Clients who have a high-traffic location can gain a lot of insight into what their customers are doing in their business location. However, if you are a brand with products, your discovery of people talking about you will be a bit harder. You will have to make your branded hashtag well known so that it gets used.

1,026 likes
wearseesnap The best thing to happen to my face since botox. Just kidding, never had botox. | Nordic Skin Peel by @skyniceland
view all 33 comments

Figure 4.4. Influencer @wearseesnap has over 124K followers.

On Instagram, everyone is an influencer. Some users just have more influence than others. Well-known Instagram accounts include not only celebrities but also people who have made themselves insta-famous by posting funny content, incredible pictures of food, great outfits, beautiful home decor, puppies, or provocative pictures. These niche accounts are growing and gaining thousands of followers by the day (see Figure 4.4).

These influencers are turning their accounts into a business. There are several ways to get these influencers to post about you:

1. *Get lucky.* You have a great product and have done an incredible job marketing your business. There is a good chance that an influencer will already be a fan and will post about you. You are lucky. This is Instagram marketing gold. Regram it and ride the wave.

2. *Gift.* Reach out to influencers who appeal to the same demographic that you are trying to reach. Comment on their pictures, tweet to them, and e-mail them. Offer them the exclusive opportunity to try your product or service in exchange for a post. Depending on the size of their following, some will do this for free. However, a rising number of influencers are charging, and given the exposure that you could receive, it might be worth the splurge.

Figure 4.5. If you have a great product that an Influencer loves, that influencer may be willing to post in exchange for the product.

3. *Get creative.* Offer people an incentive to post about you. Give them access to an exclusive coupon code, something complimentary at purchase, free shipping, access to a sneak peak. The brands and personalities who win using social media are pushing the envelope and trying new things. Don't be afraid to try something new.

#Dothis

- ✓ Use appealing, eye-catching photos.

- ✓ Use relevant hashtags.

- ✓ Respond and interact with those who do so with your brand.

- ✓ Follow your competitors' followers.

- ✓ Be personal.

- ✓ Search relevant hashtags and interact with the users.

@Absolutely don't

- ✗ be overly sales-y;

- ✗ post low-res or unclear photos; or

- ✗ steal others' content without giving them photo credit.

CASE STUDY:

In late 2013 we were approached by a beauty and skin care brand that had started nine years earlier. The company had minimal success with its online sales but was mostly focused on other online retailers and boutiques. Before working with us, the company had attempted to manage its social media in-house, and since that was not the expertise of anyone in the company, efforts got little traction and had a very small following even after nine years in the market. Fortunately, the company hired us, and we immediately turned things around. We developed a strategy on Facebook, Twitter, Instagram, Pinterest, and Google+. The advertising budget was small, so we had to focus our efforts on "free" wins. The platform where we had major success was Instagram. Users on Instagram love beauty brands. We, personally, discover new products on Instagram every day. So how did we achieve these amazing results?

1. We discovered when we started working with this company that it had a very loyal fan base, but it was not providing relevant content for fans to like and share. We quickly developed a successful content strategy that included:

    - pictures behind the scenes at fashion shows

    - photo shoots of the products

    - regrams of fans using their products

    - motivational quotes

    - pictures of the founder

2. We reached out to Instagram influencers and gave them product. Accounts with 100,000+ followers were posting pictures using the beauty products. The second an influencer posted and tagged the brand, the number of followers on the account increased dramatically.

- We were very proactive and searched terms such as #beauty and #stress and started conversations with those users to develop relationships.

- We hosted several photo contests where we created brand-specific hashtags that are still being used by fans to this day.

- We coordinated cross-promotions with some of their top retailers: Birchbox, Ulta, Ipsy.

THE OUTCOME

In a year, we increased the company's following by 2,089%—from 238 to 5,209!

THE MORAL OF THE STORY

Give your fans the insight into your company that they can't get anywhere else. Our content on Instagram was exclusive to that platform, and our efforts were focused on interacting with fans and retailers. Be engaging. Be responsive. Be likeable, loveable, and followable.

CHAPTER 5

Pinterest

What it's all about, how to use it, and how to increase your website traffic and drive sales

Think of Pinterest as a digital bulletin board—today's version of clipping out recipes, ripping out photos from your favorite magazine, or even bookmarking items on your desktop. Much like Instagram, Pinterest is purely visual. The goal of Pinterest for any brand is to drive traffic to your website. Pinterest users are predominantly women—and it is often reported that these women have money to burn. So if your target demographic is women and you are an e-commerce company, then Pinterest will be your BFF.

To better understand how to use Pinterest for your business, you must first understand how the average Pinterest user uses the site. People use Pinterest to decorate their homes, plan their weddings, store their favorite festive recipes, plan trips, redesign their wardrobes, plan events, and keep track of all the things they want. It's meant to be inspirational, aspirational, and useful. So keep this in mind when you start pinning for your brand!

Setting up a Pinterest page is straightforward. By this point, you've probably noticed that most social media platforms connect with one another. While we don't recommend sending all of your pins to Facebook and Twitter, you definitely want to share the links to your website and other social media on your Pinterest profile. Once you've set up your profile, you'll be prompted to follow boards and accounts. Then it's your turn. You'll want to download the Pin It button to your web browser: just go to the help section, where there's a link for adding the button. Now, whenever consumers are on a website (most importantly yours), all they have to do is press the Pin It button and they'll automatically see all of the pinnable images from that web page. These pins will then all link back to the website where they were found whenever someone clicks on them in Pinterest (yes, that is the sound of people discovering your blog or website).

One key step in creating your business Pinterest page is verifying your website. To do this, you simply ask your web developer to include a line of code in your website (see Figure 5.1). Once the line of code is added, you go back to your Pinterest profile setting and click on **Verify Settings**. If you do this correctly, a checkmark will appear next to your website on your Pinterest profile. There are several benefits to this: (1) it shows other Pinterest users that you are a verified account and gives you more credibility, and (2) it gives you access to Pinterest Analytics, which we discuss later in the chapter.

STEP 1: CLICK ON **VERIFY WEBSITE.**

STEP 2: GIVE THE CODE TO YOUR WEB DEVELOPER.

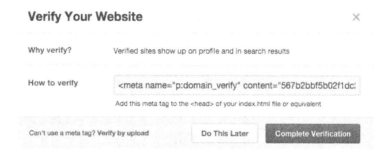

Figure 5.1. The line of code in the "How to verify" section is the code that you need to put into your website.

Now let's get to the fun part. What do you pin? Obviously, you'll want to pin your products or images from your blog posts or website. However, if you want to gain a large following, it is very important to be a part of the Pinterest community. Repin other people's pins, and pin amazing finds from around the web to curate some stylish boards that are visually appealing and help build your brand. Let's say you're a clothing company. Can you pin your favorite recipes? Absolutely! Your Pinterest boards should showcase personality and discerning taste, but they should also be far reaching in topic. The best way to get a handle on some good board ideas is to do some Pinterest stalking of your own. Did we say stalking? We meant research, of course. Find your favorite brands or big-name bloggers and see what they are pinning and repinning. The most important things to keep in mind are that visual appeal is paramount and that the pin should link back to its original source. That's just proper Pinterest etiquette.

If you're looking at your newly acquired Pinterest page, adding a board is as easy as clicking on the plus sign and **Create a Board**. Name your board with a certain topic. Don't be too broad, because you want to be able to create more boards down the line. It's fine to be cutesy when naming your board, but you also want people to discover it easily. So think about key words people will be searching. You also have the option of making "secret boards." These boards are only visible to you, the pinner. Since you're trying to build a business, there's very little about your Pinterest boards that you'll want to keep secret, but this is a good place to store pins for future projects or product launches. Whenever you're ready, click on the **Edit** button and turn off the invisibility feature. Once you do this there's no turning back, so make sure you're ready.

Pinterest is a discovery platform, where people will discover your products and services by browsing through the site and searching for specific key words. You need to keep this in mind when writing your pin descriptions. Make sure you are being as descriptive as possible. Use adjectives such as *green, shiny, glittery, soft*. You want people to find you and be excited when they click on your pin.

Pinterest is evolving as we speak, as are all the platforms. As we write this, Pinterest is testing its advertising platform, Promoted Pins. Another recent development is the tool Rich Pins. Rich Pins are pins that include more detail about a specific pin, and there are five types:

1. Place Pins

2. Article Pins

3. Product Pins

4. Recipe Pins

5. Movie Pins

These Rich Pins can be very beneficial but, unfortunately, are not for those who are not tech savvy. If you are interested in learning more, visit the business section of Pinterest. Rich Pins require setting up meta tags on your site and an application process through Pinterest.

As on all of the other social media platforms, hosting a contest is a great way to build a following and reward loyal fans on Pinterest. There are several options for running a Pinterest contest, as well as software to help you get started. Contests can be simple, such as pinning an image to one of your boards for a chance to win, or more involved, such as creating a board around a specific theme. As always, the lower the barrier of entry is, the more entries you'll get. Take a look at some Pinterest contests (search "contest" and you'll see tons) to get some ideas of what others are doing.

People often ask, "What's the secret to Pinterest?" Unfortunately, there isn't one. Building a Pinterest following takes time. Promoted Pins are now available and you can promote certain pins that drive traffic back to your website. We have had a lot of success with promoted pins from our fashion clients. You can track conversions associated with specific pins.

It's important to interact with other users, repin from other boards, comment on other people's pins, and always use key words and the best images possible to help with your search ranking.

Pinterest has recently improved its analytics section. Here's where you will find valuable insight into who is following you, which boards are the most popular, which pins have received the most clicks, and much, much more (see Figure 5.2).

Figure 5.2. Go to **Settings→ Analytics** and you'll find a wealth of information such as most popular pins, how many impressions your pins are getting, and demographic information about your followers.

One of the most important pieces of information on Pinterest is who is pinning from your website. The easiest way to check this is to go to www.Pinterest.com/source/yourwebsite.com. For example, if you want to know who is pinning from Zara, simply type in www.Pinterest.com/source/www.zara.com and see what types of clothes people have pinned most recently (see Figure 5.3 for an example). Once you know who is pinning and what they are pinning, you can go in and like these pins. This will send a notification to the person pinning from your website and, hopefully, inspire them to follow your Pinterest account if they aren't already.

Figure 5.3. Above is a screenshot of the most recent pins from Zara's website. By simply typing in www.pinterest.com/source/zara. com, anyone can see what is being pinned from the site.

#Dothis

- ✓ Pin hi-res, gorgeous photos.

- ✓ Use multiple key words and thorough descriptions, keeping search terms in mind.

- ✓ Pin directly from sources.

- ✓ Pin all of your products, blog posts, and press.

- ✓ Incorporate variety into your boards.

- ✓ Check who is pinning from your website and engage them.

- ✓ Use creative board titles using keywords that people search for.

@Absolutely don't

- ✗ pin low-quality images;

✕ change the source of other people's pins to your website; and

✕ only pin your own pins.

CASE STUDY

One of our beauty clients, a skin care line, was interested in growing online sales through the company's own e-commerce site. Because its line was also sold at retailers throughout the country, it was very important to build brand awareness and position the company's products as the go-to for all skin care needs. In building itself into a lifestyle brand, the company wanted to break into the bridal market arena.

What do you do when you want to attract brides? Pinterest is *the* place for brides. We came up with a unique hashtag, which then became the name of the contest, and developed a board creation pin-to-win with one lucky bride-to-be taking home the entire product line (to be used in preparation for her big day). The rules were simple:

- Follow the brand on Pinterest.

- Create a board with our branded title.

- Pin your dream wedding, including one skin care product to help you prep.

- Submit a link to your board.

THE OUTCOME

- Fifty-seven boards were created as entries.

- Fifty-seven-plus pins were pinned directly from the e-commerce website.

- The brand grew its Pinterest following by 68 people throughout the contest.

THE MORAL OF THE STORY

By creating a branded contest around brides and weddings, we were able to reach an entire population that the company wished to target. Because the boards were all public, we essentially had 57 brand ambassadors speaking to the alignment of the skin care line with their own wedding. The addition of pins linking back to the company's website significantly increased traffic to the site despite the relatively small number of participants. The company's products and pins also now ranked in search terms on Pinterest for wedding prep as well as skin care.

CHAPTER 6

Google+

What it is, how to use it, and why it matters more than what you may think

First, we'll go ahead and explain what Google+ is, in case you're a tad confused. Every person with a Gmail account automatically has a Google+ profile, whether you use it or not. For businesses, we recommend creating a Google+ business page. A Google+ business page is similar to a Facebook page in that there are administrators, and the page must be created from an individual's account. Click on the +[your name] at the top right of your Gmail account and see the drop-down menu below the home icon to get started creating a page (see Figure 6.1 on next page).

Google+ is a must, strictly from an SEO standpoint. Remember, at the beginning, when we went over how important it is to rank high in a Google search? Well, Google has included Google+ as a big component of this measurement. Therefore, it is imperative that you include Google+ in your social media strategy and post content there daily. This is fairly easy to do. Don't fret, ladies—this is going to be much less work than you think. You

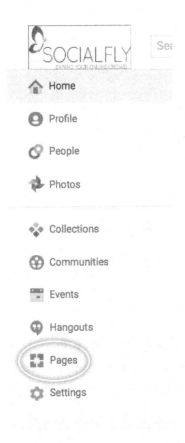

can easily repurpose the content you are using on other platforms and share it here as well. You might get called out for wearing sweatpants twice in one week, but no one is going to shame you for using the exact same post on Facebook and Google+. The only added element is hashtags. As on other social media sites, hashtagging is important here, except the hashtag will look different (see image 6.2). Make sure to hashtag whatever search terms you want your page to rank for. For example, at Socialfly we would hashtag #socialmedia, #socialmediaagency, #NYC, #business, and so on.

To post, simply type in the **Share What's New** dialogue box. Upload an image or video the exact same way you would on Facebook. The easiest way to make sure all of this gets done, though, is to schedule in advance. Google+ content can be scheduled through HootSuite, just like Twitter. If you ask your customers if they use Google+, you will probably hear many say no and others ask what it is. This can make growing your presence on the platform a challenge and is a good reason why you shouldn't spend much of your time here. While having people follow you on

Google+ is beneficial, even some of the larger brands don't own a massive following. Having users +1 your content (similar to a like and a share) can help with SEO, but it is a challenge, as not many people rely on this platform to get information and updates from businesses they frequent. Simply focus on posting consistently and keeping your business information accurate. Your Google+ page will pop up in search results, so make sure there is a link to your website, contact information, and business hours posted.

Figure 6.2. The hashtags in this post are designed for SEO purposes.

Verifying your Google+ page is also important, as it will give you access to Google Analytics, where you can see some of the results of your efforts. Your page will prompt you to verify your website, or if you have a physical location you'll be sent a postcard to make sure you are really where you say you are. If you need to verify a website, you'll get a code to send to your web developer. Once this code is placed at the back end of your website, a little checkmark will show up next to your website. Congratulations, you aren't a fake!

Once you are verified, you'll notice a section of analytics. Now you can see how many views your page is getting each month, how many clicks you are receiving, and whether you have any new reviews. If you have a physical location, you'll also get information on that, such as how many people requested driving directions to your business in the last month.

Finally, the ultimate test of your efforts on Google+ will be your search ranking. We recommend doing a monthly search of your services on Google to see where your business ranks. For example, if you own a clothing boutique in East Hampton, google "clothing stores in East Hampton" and see if you are on the first page of the results. This will take time, but consistent posting on social media has proven results in search engine optimization.

Once you set up your Google+ page, you will want to make sure that it is linked to your YouTube page. Both YouTube and Google+ are Google products, and Google has decided to link the two platforms together. This means that anything you post on your YouTube page will automatically feed Google+ as a post.

#Dothis

✓ Post daily.

✓ Repurpose your content from other social platforms.

✓ Use hashtags of key words associated with your business, particularly key words people would use to search for a business such as yours.

✓ Link to your website often.

✓ Verify your website.

@Absolutely don't

- ✗ spend a great deal of time on Google+ or

- ✗ ignore this platform.

CASE STUDY

We have always used social media to promote our own business, Socialfly. Everything we tell our clients to do, we do ourselves. One of the first things we did when we started our own business was create our own social media strategy. Our goal was to position ourselves as knowledgeable experts in the social media space and attract clients. Fortunately, when we started, Google had changed its algorithm and was giving more weight to websites that embraced social—a very lucky thing for a very social social media agency such as ours. Early on, our strategy included the use of Google+. We employed all of the tactics that we explained earlier in this chapter.

THE OUTCOME

After several months, our social media agency ranked on the first page of Google searches on "social media agency" or "social media agency NYC." Ever since we climbed to the first page of Google with those key words, we have been getting leads from our website and have landed the large clients we wanted to attract through our efforts.

THE MORAL OF THE STORY

People always ask us, how did you get on the first page of Google? Our answer: by sticking to our social media strategy. It is very important to actively post to Google+, as it is a Google product and will directly impact your SEO. It's less important to worry about attracting a huge circle of followers or worrying about engagement on the page.

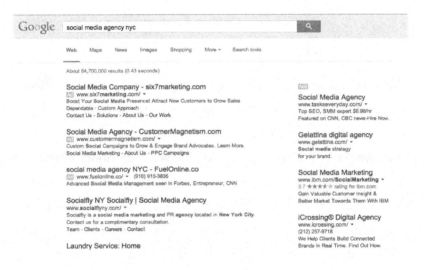

CHAPTER 7

LinkedIn

Why you should have a profile, how it should be optimized, and best practices

Every entrepreneur or woman in business should have a LinkedIn profile. It is an absolute must, these days, for a few important reasons:

- It is your digital resume and a way for you to potentially land your client.

- It is a great way to keep in touch, professionally, with people you meet at networking events.

- It is a great way to find new talent for your business or land your next new client.

We have made many strategic connections on LinkedIn, and every day, we hear wonderful success stories. The key to LinkedIn is being an active user. It's not enough to simply set up a profile and hope people find you, and LinkedIn is not the place to stalk old friends. You'll notice right away that there is an option for a premium (paid) account, which we'll talk about a little later, but there's plenty you can do with a free account, so don't let that stand in your way.

YOUR PROFILE

LinkedIn is online networking at its finest. So, as with any great event, you want to make sure that you—via your profile—look the part. Start with the obvious and put in your full name. This is like an online business card, so you want it to match whatever you're going to be handing out. You also want to secure a vanity URL (a unique web address that you can direct people to and put on your business card). In the bottom left corner it will give you the option to edit the address that begins with www.linkedin.com/in/. Try to get your name or some variant of it as the ending. Next, upload a professional photo. Save the selfies, the bikini shots, and the photo of you and your boyfriend for Facebook and Instagram. Here you want a clean headshot that is representative of the type of businesswoman you are. You now have the option for a cover photo as well. Here you'll want to highlight your business or show a bit of personality, but again, save the group shots of you and your friends for other social networks.

It's extremely important to fill out all sections of your profile and to leave your settings on "public." This isn't Facebook, and you won't be sharing personal information, so the more eyes on your business history, the better. You want to include all previous positions, your education, and the summary section, as well as hobbies, charities you are involved in, and interests. Think of your profile as an online resume. LinkedIn differs from a resume in that there's room for a little personality and extra info. People tend to think that they should only focus on their current role, but that shuts the door to so many possible connections. On LinkedIn, people are searching for ways to make connections—beyond just a name and a face. Organizations you are involved with, charities you are passionate about, where you went to school, your sorority, and your interests are prime examples of places to stand out from the crowd. Speaking of which, there is a crowd—over 364 million registered users as of first quarter of 2015. Setting up a standout profile is a crucial first step in joining the masses of people using LinkedIn to their advantage.

The summary section often stumps people, but you don't want to skip it. Don't think of it as a cover letter, because it should be much more personal. It's totally fine to use the first person singular case. The summary is the space where you want to highlight your story in one or two paragraphs. As an entrepreneur, you'll also want to showcase your business. Go ahead and tell people what's so amazing about the services or products you provide. Look up people in similar industries that you admire and see how they have written their summary section. Some are more creative than others, but at the very least, this is your elevator pitch of why people should want to connect with you (see Figure 7.1 as an example of a summary section).

 Summary

Stephanie Abrams is the Co-Founder and CEO of Socialfly, a social media marketing and public relations agency located in New York City. In addition to offering traditional public relations outreach, Socialfly focuses on developing social media marketing strategies designed to improve brand awareness, lead generation, and reputation management. Specializing in beauty, fashion, and hospitality, Socialfly has worked with several national brands including: John Varvatos, Michael C Fina, Nest Fragrances, Cinda B and Caviar Russe.

A graduate of the Cornell University School of Hotel Administration, Stephanie began her professional career in sales at Marriott International. Recognizing the tremendous opportunity social media presented businesses from a sales and marketing perspective while helping some entrepreneurial friends, Stephanie launched her first social media agency, Gabbaroo, in 2009. Since then, she has helped hundreds of businesses enhance and successfully leverage their online presence through fan engagement and interaction. She has appeared on Bloomberg TV's Taking Stock, and is a regular contributor on Entrepreneur.com.

In addition to her work at Socialfly, Stephanie is also the Co-Founder of the female entrepreneurial networking group, Startups in Stilettos, which connects young female professionals and entrepreneurs through social networking events. Having been diagnosed in 2011, she is a champion of Multiple Sclerosis awareness and fundraising, and is a member of the National Multiple Sclerosis Society's Marketing and Corporate Relations Committee. She is currently working on completing her first book, designed to teach female entrepreneurs how to successfully use social media to grow their businesses.

For more information please contact Steph@SociaflyNY.com

Specialties: Social Media Consulting, Social Media Strategy Creation, Digital Marketing, Hospitality Sales & Marketing

Figure 7.1

The last few items on your profile are easy to skip over, but once again, it's important to be thorough. Add your skills. Be accurate, but don't be shy either. You'll notice many people have a long skills section, and you want to be sure to paint a broad picture of your skills as an employee and business owner. Then, join relevant groups and follow interesting companies (most importantly your own, and if your business doesn't have a LinkedIn page yet, never fear; we'll explain how to do that too).

Once you are fully dressed—that is, when your profile looks complete—it's time to start mingling! Having a lot of connections is important, but it's even more important to have quality connections. When you first set up your profile, you'll be prompted to connect through your e-mail contacts, and that's a great way to get started. Make sure you are connected to the obvious people— anyone who works with you or is in your immediate networking circles and groups. After you have this initial base of connections, it's a good rule of thumb to send a personalized message before connecting with new people or those you haven't spoken to in years. Remind them where you met and how you might be able to do business together in the future. Keep it short, but open up the dialogue for conversation.

Another way to enhance your profile and interact with your connections is through endorsements. You can endorse anyone you are connected to for the skills listed on that person's profile. You may also suggest other skills. Often, endorsing people for a skill is a good way to have them endorse you in return. "Recommendations"—the section at the very bottom of your profile—is another great way to stand out. It's like offering references before someone even asks. Reach out to past or current bosses or supervisors you've kept in touch with and trusted colleagues and ask if they might write a recommendation for you. On LinkedIn, it's good practice to do for others what you would appreciate them doing in return. If you have a stellar intern or former employee, offer to write a recommendation to really help make that person's profile shine.

You'll notice that when you look at another person's profile, it will state whether that person is a first-, second-, or third-degree connection. First-degree connections are people you are already linked to. You can send messages to these people and view their entire profile. These should be people you know. A second-degree connection means that someone you are already connected to knows this person. This is some of the most valuable information that LinkedIn provides. When you are looking for a job, an employee, or a company to do business with, finding a second-degree connection is an amazing first step. LinkedIn will identify people you know who are connected to this person, and from there, you can ask for an introduction. Don't simply ask to connect because your BFF knows them. Take the time to have your BFF personally introduce you—whether that's via e-mail or on LinkedIn. Third-degree connections are harder to get to, as these are people with whom you don't share any connections. This doesn't mean that you can't reach out to them on LinkedIn, but it's just like being at a party: people will be much more inclined to join in a conversation if you have a mutual point of contact.

Besides making connections, there are other ways to stay active on your personal profile. Follow companies and join groups. You can follow magazines, news services, and organizations that you work with. Some groups are open to the public while membership of others is by invitation only. If you are invited to a group, let's say, Female Entrepreneurs, it's important to be an active part of discussions. If you are an expert on a subject matter, let's say, social media, it's important to join groups and discussions that are taking place and give your opinion. This is a good way for people outside your connections to discover you and your business. Finally, you can share status updates. This is *not* the place to give people the rundown of your day. It's not the place to share political opinions, engagement announcements, or any other type of personal information. Status updates should be relevant to your business or your personal brand. Share an interesting article in your field. Share links to your new website or portfolio. Announce that you are looking to hire.

In 2014, LinkedIn also rolled out a "publishing platform." Now anyone can write blog posts that appear on LinkedIn. If you are already a contributing blogger somewhere, this is a great place to repurpose that content. Your published posts will appear in the LinkedIn Pulse section and on your connection's home news feed. The more quality content and engaging posts you write, the greater your chances are of becoming one of the "recommended" stories that show up in people's feeds. Catchy titles to your blog post are always recommended, and you want to be sure to tag your post with relevant key words so that LinkedIn pushes out your content to the right people. Figure 7.2 shows Stephanie Abrams Cartin's published posts.

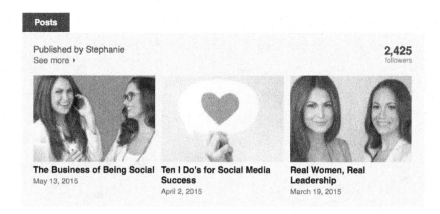

Figure 7.2

Now, is paying for a Premium account really worth it? It depends on how much you plan on using the platform to actively generate leads. The main difference between a Premium account and a regular one is that you can send InMail to someone you aren't connected to. InMail is LinkedIn's interplatform e-mail; it is like a Facebook messaging system. If you are looking to connect with new business, this can be a way in the door rather than searching for an e-mail address. A Premium account also shows you more information about who has been looking at your profile.

As an entrepreneur, your LinkedIn activity should be strategic and consistent. You'll get the most out of your personal profile, but you should also set up a page for your business. People can follow your business page for status updates, general information, and job postings. Job postings are one of the most important reasons to have a company page. As for other company content, we suggest strategically posting Facebook content to this platform. Reserve the most informational, content-based posts for LinkedIn, and save the lighthearted, fun posts for Facebook and Instagram. Once you have a page established, encourage all of your employees to follow the account and make sure all of your personal and company blog post links are also posted here.

Figure 7.3. Here's an example of a business page on LinkedIn. On the right-hand side you'll see how you are connected to the company (if you happen to be connected to someone who works there) and a number of the employees at the particular business who have LinkedIn profiles.

One thing to note about setting up a business page (and this goes for all of the social media channels we have talked about) is that you want to make sure the owner and manager is you (or a cofounder). We have run into multiple examples of official pages that are set up by an employee who then leaves. It's very difficult to gain ownership rights back from an employee you can't track down. However, as on other platforms, you'll have the option of setting up others as managers, who can then handle the daily posting.

Finally, as you've seen with all other social media platforms, LinkedIn has begun an advertising platform for businesses. If you are looking to get your job postings out there or even to raise awareness for your business, you can pay for views. If your business is B2B, then LinkedIn advertising can work for you to attract new clients.

#Dothis

- ✓ Spend time completing your profile in detail.
- ✓ Include a headline.
- ✓ Keep your profile updated to reflect any new titles or positions.
- ✓ Create a vanity URL.
- ✓ Include links to your profile in your e-mail signature and on business cards.
- ✓ Comment on posts and join discussions.
- ✓ Publish original content as posts.
- ✓ Ask for introductions to your second-degree connections.
- ✓ Endorse others for their skills.
- ✓ Ask for recommendations from trusted colleagues, business partners, and clients.
- ✓ Upgrade to a premium account if you plan on reaching out to people you are not connected to.
- ✓ Turn your LinkedIn contacts whom you have not met in person into real meetings or phone calls.
- ✓ Download the LinkedIn app so that you can continue to connect when you are on the go.

@Absolutely don't

- ✗ post unprofessional comments or photos;
- ✗ lie on your resume or exaggerate the facts;

✗ send invitations to connect with people you don't know without some type of message;

✗ ignore your inbox or pending invitations; and

✗ keep your profile settings on private.

CASE STUDY

We have used LinkedIn extensively for Socialfly. Our main goals for using LinkedIn are:

- build a network of potential strategic partners

- connect with marketing directors at the brands we want to work with

- recruit top talent

- position ourselves as social media experts

To achieve these goals, we employ the following tactics:

- We go to a lot of networking events, and when we do, we make sure to connect with the people we meet on LinkedIn to continue the conversation. There are so many instances in the history of our business where we have overcome challenges by tapping into the resources we have built over the years.

- We often put together lists of ideal clients we would like to work with. Our next step is always to check LinkedIn for people we know who work at those companies. We are not shy when it comes to asking people we know to connect us with the people we want to meet. This is the beauty of LinkedIn. It is a public Rolodex that you can use to your advantage. There have been many instances where this tactic has landed us our next new client.

- When using LinkedIn as a recruiting tool, we do the following:

    - We post the job listings to our personal accounts.

    - We post social media news, our blog updates, and open job listings on our company page. Over time, we have acquired many LinkedIn followers who engage with the posts we share.

- The LinkedIn publishing tool has been a tremendous resource for us. We typically share our blog content, and our posts reach thousands of people organically.

THE OUTCOME

We have generated new business from LinkedIn leads as well as helped connect people in our network with each other. We have published blog posts that have over 4000 organic views per post, which is more brand awareness. In addition, we know that LinkedIn drives traffic to our website, also helping with our SEO.

THE MORAL OF THE STORY

LinkedIn is yet another platform to help with your general social media efforts and increase traffic to your website. It is also an extremely important personal branding tool that can allow you to stay connected with all those people you meet at your in-person networking events.

CHAPTER 8

Metrics

How to measure all of your hard work

You made it to this chapter, which means you now have a good understanding of what you need to do to achieve your social media goals. But you might still be wondering:

- How long will it take me to grow my following?

- How do I know my Facebook Ads are working?

- Was my contest successful?

- Is my content interesting enough?

- When will the phones start ringing off the hook and sales double?

These are all great questions, and we're glad you asked. Every good social media strategy needs goals and metrics to measure progress. Some key performance indicators to pay attention to and track on a weekly basis are:

FACEBOOK PAGE

- How many new people like the page? During what time frame?

- Were there spikes in likes on specific days?

- How many people are you reaching each week?

FACEBOOK CONTENT

- Which posts get the most likes, comments, and shares?

- Did you pay to boost those posts? Whom did you target?

- How many people did you reach with your posts?

- Which posts did not generate engagement?

- How many people clicked on your link?

FACEBOOK ADS

- What is your cost per like? Per click? Per conversion? Per engagement? Is this cost more or less than the previous week?

- How many people have seen your ad?

- How many times have people seen your ad? What is the frequency?

- What is your click-through rate?

You can find this information in the Facebook Ads Manager as well as on the Insights page.

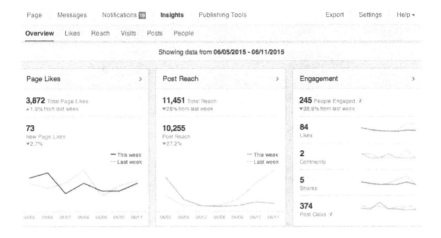

Figure 8.1. This is the Insights section of Facebook, available to any admin on the page. From here you can see how many people are seeing and interacting with your posts. You can also find out more information about the people that like your page. You'll see graphs which show your page's growth over time, as well as likes on the page.

TWITTER

- How many people are seeing your tweets?

- Are your tweets getting any retweets, replies, or favorites?

- Which types of tweets get the most engagement?

- How many new followers are you getting per day?

- Have you connected with any influencers?

- How many mentions do you get per day?

- How often do you respond to questions?

- How many accounts are you following per day?

You can find this information via Twitter.com in the Twitter Analytics section.

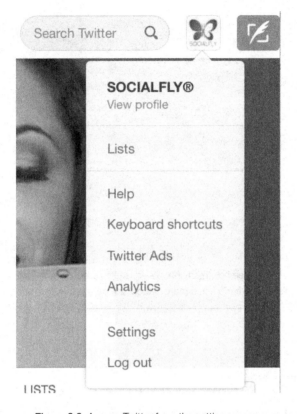

Figure 8.2. Access Twitter from the settings menu.

INSTAGRAM

- How many followers do you have?

- How many new followers are you getting per day?

- What % of people are following you back?

- Are other people talking about you?

- How many people are using your brand-specific hashtag?

- Which posts get the most engagement?

- Are the comments on your post positive?

You can find this information on Iconosquare.

PINTEREST

- How many followers do you have?

- How many people are pinning from your site?

- How many people are you following per day?

- Are people repinning your content?

You can find this information on Pinterest.com.

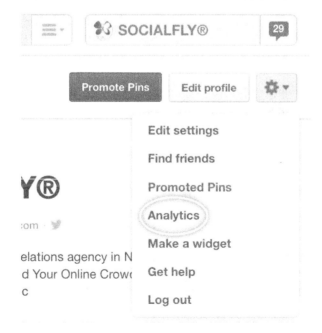

WEBSITE TRAFFIC

- Based on Google Analytics results, is your traffic from social media increasing?

- Which social media platforms generate the most traffic?

- What types of content generate the most traffic?

- Are people making purchases from your site? Which platforms are the most influential?

You can find this information on Google Analytics.

Insights for your business, last 30 days

Insights · 46.9K 17%↓ Views · 667 7%↑ Clicks · 2 33%↓ New followers · View insights

E-MAILS

- How many e-mail addresses are you collecting from social?

- How many e-mail addresses did you collect from your contest?

- What is your open rate (percentage of people actually reading the e-mails you send) from the e-mails you collected through social?

You can find this information via your e-mail marketing software (we recommend MailChimp).

REVIEWS

- Are people giving positive reviews or negative reviews?

- Are you responding to all reviews?

- Are you receiving similar feedback over and over? If so, what can you learn from this?

STORE/LOCATION VISITS

- Are more people coming to visit your location?

- How are people finding out about you?

- Are you getting more phone calls and e-mails?

OVERALL SALES

- Are your overall sales up from this time last year/since you started using social media?

These are all factors to consider when evaluating whether or not your social media efforts are successful. Everything should be tied back to your initial goals. Remember, social media takes time. We usually tell our clients that it takes six months to really see an impact. The more effort you put in, the more you will get out of it. If your following is not growing each day, you are doing something wrong and should reevaluate your social media strategy.

CHAPTER 9

Recommended Social Media Management Tools

What we use to make our jobs easier

Social media is a full-time job. For some large companies, it can occupy up to 100 full-time jobs. It is very labor intensive and requires both creative and analytical minds. We always say that people can spot automation a mile off, but even so, there are some websites and tools that you can use to help manage and monitor your social media efforts. Below is a collection of some of our personal favorites:

HOOTSUITE

This is a great management tool that allows you to see all of your social media pages in one place. You can easily respond and comment on all your social media platforms. This is especially great for scheduling content on Google+ and LinkedIn.

CROWDFIRE

As we mentioned in chapter 5, following people is a common tactic for getting followers. However, you want to make sure that you unfollow those who do not follow you back. Crowdfire can give you this information for Instagram, and you can unfollow users directly from the app. When you unfollow people, it is very important to be extremely strategic and also mindful of who you are unfollowing. People tend to take "unfollows" very personally. You can also use Crowdfire for Twitter as well.

WOOBOX

Running contests on your page is a must for some brands. You can do this easily and cost-effectively by using a platform called Woobox. Woobox charges are based on the number of fans you have, so be sure to buy it when you are first starting your page so that you can have the lowest tiered pricing.

OFFERPOP

Another option for managing your social media contests is Offerpop. It is easy to use, and its contests are very visually appealing.

SIMPLY MEASURED

A great tool for insights and analytics, Simply Measured provides information that can be more valuable and easy to understand than the insights available on the Twitter and Facebook platforms. It will also tell you who your main brand advocates are.

SOCIAL BAKERS

We love this tool and suggest using it if you want to take a deeper dive into your social media metrics.

ICONOSQUARE

We use Iconosquare to monitor our Instagram efforts. Here, you can learn how many new followers you get over a certain period of time, which filters get the most likes, and which fans like your pictures the most.

Our Final Words of Wisdom

We'd *like* to offer you a few last words of wisdom, but we'd also love for you to follow us on our social media platforms so that you can stay up to date on all the latest in the constantly changing world of social media and reach out to us if you ever need a little more hands-on help. We are always one tweet away, and we love connecting and chatting with savvy entreprenistas like you.

If you're first starting out or trying to grow a business, social media must be a part of your marketing strategy. Sometimes, it will be your little black dress, the staple that makes you feel good. Other times, it might feel a little flashy—such as the stilettos you're not so sure you can get away with. Some of it may seem complicated, and some of it may even seem unnecessary, but think of us as friends telling you, "That jacket was made for you!" As entreprenistas, we know this: if you leverage social media correctly, you'll have no buyer's remorse.

Follow Socialfly

- ✓ Facebook.com/Socialfly
- ✓ Twitter.com/Socialfly
- ✓ Instagram.com/Socialfly
- ✓ linkedin.com/company/socialfly

Follow Courtney

- ✓ Twitter.com/CourtSpritzer
- ✓ Instagram.com/CourtSpritzer
- ✓ LinkedIn.com/courtneyspritzer

Follow Stephanie

- ✓ Twitter.com/stephjillabrams
- ✓ Instagram.com/stephjillabrams
- ✓ LinkedIn.com/stephjillabrams

9 781599 326351